The Internet for W

Using the new medium to research,
promote and publish your work

Internet Handbooks

Books & Publishing on the Internet
Chat on the Internet
Creating a Business in Cyberspace
Email for Beginners
Finding a Job on the Internet
Free Stuff on the Net
Gardens & Gardening on the Internet
History on the Internet
Homes & Property on the Internet
Law & Lawyers on the Internet
Personal Finance on the Internet
The Internet for Schools
The Internet for Students
The Internet for Writers
Maths on the Internet
News & Magazines on the Internet
Personal Finance on the Internet
Shops & Shopping on the Internet
Travel & Holidays on the Internet
Wildlife & Conservation on the Internet

Other titles in preparation

The Internet for Writers

Using the new medium to
research, promote and publish your work

Nick Daws

BSc (Hons)
Member of the Society of Authors

Internet Handbooks

First published in 1999 by Internet Handbooks, a Division of International
Briefings Ltd, Plymbridge House, Estover Road, Plymouth PL6 7PY,
United Kingdom.
Telephone: (01752) 202301. Fax: (01752) 202331

Series web site: http://www.internet-handbooks.co.uk
Customer services: cservs@plymbridge.com
Editorial email: publisher@internet-handbooks.co.uk

Produced for Internet Handbooks by Deer Park Productions.

Typeset by PDQ Typesetting, Newcastle-under-Lyme

Printed and bound by The Cromwell Press Ltd, Trowbridge, Wiltshire.

Contents

. . . .

Illustrations list

Preface

Writers today are doubly fortunate. First, we have the benefit of word processors, which cut drastically the time needed to revise a piece of work (remember the days of passing endless drafts through the typewriter, when all you really wanted to do was change a couple of paragraphs?). And now we have the advantage of the second greatest invention of the twentieth century as far as writers are concerned – the internet.

You could almost believe the net was designed for writers, so many benefits does it offer. First and foremost, the internet opens the doors to a vast, almost infinite, store of human knowledge. Much of this is available free (or at least very cheaply) from your desktop. All you need to get access to it is a computer, a modem and a contract with an internet service provider. Then all that wonderful information will be instantly on hand whenever you require it.

That is by no means the whole of it. Through email the net offers a quick, cheap and easy way to communicate with other writers and editors. You can set up a 'home page' on the web and use this to promote yourself and your writing to a world-wide audience for literally just a few pounds a month. The web itself is a vast new market for writers. Every one of the millions of web sites has at least some writing on it – and some sites are devoted entirely to writing and publishing. All this is there for you on the internet, and much more besides.

Admittedly, it's not all plain sailing (or surfing). No-one owns or controls the net. It has therefore developed in a haphazard way, and is all rather sprawling and chaotic. One writer has compared the internet to a huge library in which someone has turned out all the lights and scattered the card indexes across the floor. At times the net undoubtedly has a 'wild frontier' feeling to it. This is not helped by the fact that the uses to which some individuals have put the technology would not be regarded as universally desirable . . .

Even so, there is no doubt that every writer working today can benefit from the internet. And just a year or two down the line, having net access is likely to become not just a valuable asset but an essential. Editors and publishers will expect you to have email and web facilities, just as they might expect a fax machine now. Even today, if you're not online, you risk missing out on many work opportunities.

My aim by the time you have read this book is that you will have a good basic understanding of the internet and the services it offers. However, I have tried to avoid the trap of producing yet another 'Introduction to the internet'. Rather than a general overview, I have

Preface ....

tried to present the subject very much from a writer's viewpoint. I hope that by the time you have finished the book, you will have discovered at least half a dozen ways in which the internet could help you with your work. And when you get on-line – if you're not already – I hope that visiting the web sites and following up the other resources mentioned here will inspire you with more ideas still.

Although I hope this book will reach a wide readership, I have tried to counter the US-dominated flavour of most books on the internet. You will therefore find listed plenty of sites and services based in the UK and other parts of the world, alongside the usual (and often excellent) American resources.

I do hope you enjoy reading this book as much as I have enjoyed researching and writing it. If you have any comments or suggestions for the next edition, I should be very grateful if you would send them to me c/o my publishers:

publisher@internet-handbooks.co.uk

Happy surfing, and good writing.

Nick Daws

1 Introduction

In this chapter you will discover how to:

▶ *get connected to the internet*
▶ *send and receive email*
▶ *access a newsgroup*
▶ *surf the world wide web*
▶ *observe good netiquette*

. . . .

The basics

Let's begin by answering the most basic question of all – what is the internet? As the name suggests, it is an **inter**national **net**work of computers linked up to exchange information. The internet (known as the **net** for short) began in America, and is still US dominated. However, it is not under the control of any particular government or agency.

At the heart of the internet is a set of large, powerful computers which are permanently connected to one another. Other computers, such as the one on your desk, can dial in via a phone line. Once connected they have access to information stored on many thousands of computers across the world.

For writers the internet offers numerous benefits. Perhaps the most obvious is the help it can provide with research. With an internet connection you have access to vast amounts of information. You can also check library catalogues, order books from online bookshops, send email (electronic mail) to experts in other countries, and so on – all from your home or office, for the price of a local phone call.

Apart from research, the internet offers many other benefits to a writer. Once you have an internet connection, you will have a convenient, low-cost way of:

▷ communicating with other writers and publishers

▷ marketing yourself and your work

▷ polishing your writing skills

▷ finding writing jobs and opportunities

▷ broadening your writing horizons

▷ and much, much more!

Getting online ···

These and other benefits will be explored throughout this book. But first of all, you need to get connected.

Getting online

To get on to the internet and start enjoying its many benefits, you will need three things:

1. a computer

2. a modem (a device which enables a computer to communicate with others via a phone line)

3. an account with an internet access provider

Virtually any combination of these will allow you to get on to the internet. However, at very slow speeds the experience may be more frustrating than enlightening. Let's look at the above ingredients in more detail to see what you are likely to need in practice.

The computer you will need

Most computers sold over the last few years will cope with electronic mail (email). However, if you intend to use the facilities of the world wide web – the largest and most technologically sophisticated part of the Internet – you will need something fairly modern. The minimum you will require is an IBM-compatible 486 computer or a Macintosh 68030 series with at least eight megabytes of **RAM**. RAM stands for random access memory – it is the memory a computer uses for temporary storage, like human short-term memory. The bigger this memory, the more tasks the computer can manage at the same time.

The modem you will need

A modem is a device which enables your computer to communicate with others via a phone line. Many computers sold today have modems built in, but failing this you will need to buy one. If you are buying a modem, here are three pieces of advice:

1. Get an external modem rather than internal. External modems are slightly more expensive, but they are much easier to fit – all you have to do is plug them in to the back of your computer. They also have a row of lights on them which tell you if anything is happening. With an external modem, if most of the lights suddenly go out you will know at a glance that your internet connection has been broken.

2. Get one which is as fast as possible. Modem speed is expressed in bits per second (bps). The lowest you should consider is 14,400 bps, while 28,800 is a more realistic minimum, and 56,000 is set to become the new standard.

3. Ensure that your modem is also suitable for sending faxes and data. The great majority of those sold today are suitable, but it pays to check. Even if you have a dedicated fax machine already, the facility to send and receive faxes directly from your computer can be very useful.

Your internet access provider

Unfortunately you can't just dial into the internet from your computer. You need to open an account with an internet access provider (IAP for short). Your IAP will give you an email address and connect you with the world wide web and other networks such as newsgroups.

There is a wide range of IAPs vying for your custom. Most charge a monthly subscription, and some a joining fee as well. Many allow unlimited access for your monthly fee. Some, however, charge by the hour (though the basic fee may include a certain number of 'free' hours every month). In addition, of course, there will be ordinary phone bills to pay. Some of the most popular Internet service providers, with contact details for further information, are shown in Figure 1.

Company	Telephone	Web Page
AOL	0800 279 1234	www.uk.aol.com
BT Internet	0800 800 001	www.btinternet.com
CIX	0845 355 9050	www.cix.co.uk
ClaraNET	0800 358 2828	www.clara.net
CompuServe	0990 000 200	www.compuserve.-
co.uk		
Demon	0181 371 1234	www.demon.net
Direct Connection	0800 072 0000	www.dircon.net
Enterprise	01624 677666	www.enterprise.net
FreeDotNet	0181 938 3338	www.thefree.net
Global Internet	0870 909 8041	www.global.net.uk
Microsoft (MSN)	0345 002 000	www.uk.msn.com
NetDirect	0181 293 7000	www.netdirect.net.uk
U-Net	0845 3000448	www.u-net.net
UUNET (Pipex Dial)	0500 567 000	www.uk.uu.net
Virgin Net	0500 558 800	www.virgin.net
Zetnet Services	01595 696 667	www.zetnet.co.uk

Fig. 1. Table of internet access providers.

IAPs vary widely in their terms and range of services offered. It is therefore important to weigh up carefully the options before making your choice. If you intend to make only occasional use of the internet – using it mainly for email, perhaps – a provider charging by the hour may be best. On the other hand, once you start accessing the internet for more than three or four hours a month, the hourly charges of these providers can swiftly add up. You may then be better off with a provider which charges a flat monthly fee.

Connecting up . . . .

Another important consideration is the phone number you have to call to get internet access. If at all possible, choose a provider you can call with a number in your local telephone area. Then all calls via the internet service, whether to your next-door-neighbour or a university on the other side of the world, will be charged at the same local phone rate. Most IAPs now offer 100% UK coverage at local rates, but some smaller services may only be accessible by a local call if you live in their area.

When deciding which IAP to join, give some consideration to the level of service you can expect. For example, all IAPs offer a helpline (normally free), though those of the larger ones tend to be open longer hours each day. Before signing up with your chosen IAP, try phoning their helpline at various times of the day to see how accessible (and helpful) it really is.

Reliability is also important: at busy times some IAPs become swamped with people trying to log on, with the result that the service becomes slow and unreliable. This is one area where smaller IAPs often perform better than large ones. Performance varies from month to month. To find out which IAPs are currently doing best, consult the performance tables in the monthly *Internet* magazine (available from W.H. Smith's and most larger newsagents).

There are more than 200 internet access providers in the UK today, and more than 10,000 world wide. If you are concerned about your right to privacy in the UK, or curious to find out more, you can explore internet access providers world wide at this impressive 'list of lists'. With falling phone rates, the world is potentially your oyster:

http://www.herbison.com/herbison/iap_meta_list.html

Connecting up

Having chosen your IAP, connecting up should be straightforward. Your IAP will have provided the necessary software, either on floppy disk or CD-ROM. All you need do is follow the instructions provided with this to install it on your machine.

As the software installs, you will be prompted to enter items of information. These questions are generally quite straightforward. They are designed to tell your computer whom you are joining up with and how to connect with them; but if you are confused on any point, the IAP will have a phone number for any queries about the installation procedure. This number may be different from the usual helpline number. Once your software is safely installed, you are all set to start exploring the information superhighway.

Your questions answered

What is the difference between an internet access provider and an internet service provider?

An internet service provider gives users a range of services in addition to internet access. An Internet access provider provides access only. All ISPs are also IAPs, but the reverse is not the case. To avoid confusion, this book uses the term internet access provider (IAP) throughout.

How much will it all cost?

At the time of writing the average cost of an account with an Internet access provider is around £10 a month. In addition, of course, there will be phone bills to pay. If you take full advantage of discount schemes such as BT's 'Friends and Family', you should be able to access the internet for around 1p a minute off-peak.

Which IAP offers the best value for money?

Prices are constantly changing. To assess the current situation, look at any of the monthly news-stand magazines devoted to the internet. If you are on a tight budget, a new access provider, FreeDotNet, is worth considering. They will provide two years' access for a minimum fee of just £30. An even more recent entrant to this market is FreeServe, from high street electrical store Dixons (who also own the PC World stores). Their service is free, but calls to their technical support line are charged at a premium rate.

Using email

Email is the most basic of internet services and by far the most widely used. It provides a simple method for exchanging messages and files with other internet users. These people could be on the next street or the other side of the world. The main benefits of this to you are (a) the low cost, and (b) the speed of delivery (compared with conventional mail services).

All internet access providers include software enabling you to send and receive email as part of their start-up package. They will also give you one or more email addresses. **Multiple email addresses** can be useful if you want to have separate mailboxes for other members of your family, or other departments of your business empire.

You can also get free email on the world wide web from various providers, for example Hotmail at:

http://hotmail.msn.co.uk

Of course, you will still need internet access to use this facility. However, it means you will be able to send and receive emails from *any* computer with web access – for example, at a hotel, an employer or client's premises, or a friend's home.

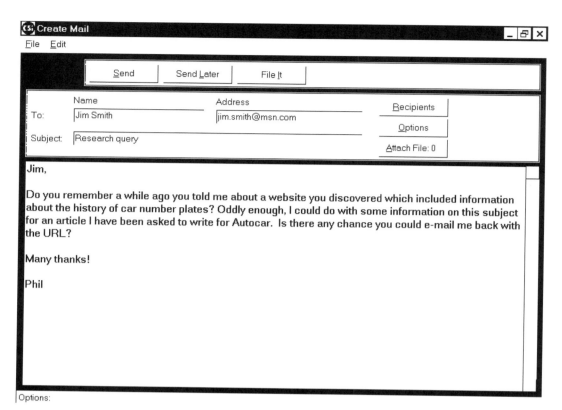

Fig. 2. An email written in CompuServe.

Sending an email

Writing and sending an email is simplicity itself. The method varies between programs, but CompuServe is typical. From the CompuServe desktop you click on *Mail Centre*, then *Create/New* to produce a new message. Type the recipient's name and email address in the appropriate boxes, then write your message.

Once your email is written, click the *Send* button, and away your message will go to its intended recipient. You can send an email to anyone you want – from the US President to your next-door neighbour – just as long as you know their internet email address.

You can send an email to two or more recipients simultaneously. You can also send electronic 'carbon copies' of your email to anyone you think might be interested. Try, however, to avoid the temptation to send multiple copies of emails just because it *is* so easy (see the section on **netiquette** later in this chapter).

Understanding email addresses

All email addresses take the following form:

username@domain.name

The **user name** is unique to each individual. The **domain name** is the address of the access provider they are connected through. So if Rachel Johnston has an AOL (America On-Line) account, her chosen email address might be:

> rachel.johnston@aol.com

If you want to send Rachel an email, you enter the above details in the address field of your email program. When you log on to send your message, this is what happens:

1. The message is transmitted via your modem and phone line to your access provider.

2. The message arrives at your access provider's mail server. (A **server** is a powerful computer capable of handling data from a range of sources simultaneously. As the name suggests, a **mail server** is one wholly dedicated to processing email.) Your access provider's mail server then uses the Internet Domain Name Service (DNS) to locate the mail server which accepts mail for the recipient's domain. In the case of a message sent to Rachel, this will be the AOL mail server.

3. Your access provider's mail server sends your message to the AOL mail server. This, in turn, directs the email to the mailbox for AOL user name rachel.johnston.

4. Here your email waits until the next time Rachel logs on. When she does, she sees that an email from you is waiting in her mailbox. Assuming she wishes to see what you have to say, she downloads the email and reads it.

Most access providers supply an **off-line mailer**. This is a program which enables you to create and store messages in your own time. Then, when you next log in, all your messages can be transmitted and incoming mail placed in your mailbox to be read when you come off-line. All this can be done in a few seconds of telephone contact. This makes email not only cheaper than the post, but also cheaper than faxes and ordinary phone calls. What's more, it takes almost the same amount of time to contact 1, 2 or 50 people with a single message.

Receiving your email

Whenever you log on, a message on screen will show you whether you have any unread messages and how many. You can then:

▷ leave them in the mailbox for another time if you're in a hurry

▷ download them into your in-tray, to be read offline

▷ read them there and then (and reply if you wish)

Many IAPs place an upper limit on the number of messages you can have in your mailbox at any time (typically 100). You should therefore aim to empty your box at reasonably regular intervals. If you are going away and have no means of getting to your mail, send a message to your most frequent contacts asking if they will avoid emailing you until your return.

File attachment ....

Your email program may also include a facility called an **auto responder**. This can be set up to reply automatically to any incoming email with a message informing the sender of your absence.

Limitations of email

Internet email uses ASCII code. ASCII stands for American Standard Code for Information Interchange. It is a simple, basic language which nearly all computers can read and understand. This means it does not support word processing features such as italics, bold or underlining. If you want to give a word or phrase in an email extra emphasis, one widely-used solution is to put an asterisk each side *like this*. Alternatively you can use underscores _like this_ to show that the word or words are underlined.

Another slight drawback with internet email is that the ASCII character set does not include a pound (£) sign. In emails, therefore, you should either write out the word 'pounds' in full, or use the widely accepted abbreviation UKP (United Kingdom pounds). Another option is to prefix the amount with a letter 'L'. For example L500 means £500.

Fig. 3 An email with file attachment. The file name of the attachment is skating.doc, showing that it is a Word file. Click on it to read it.

Sending a file attachment

As mentioned earlier, a standard email is limited to basic ASCII text. This means that you cannot send files created using other applications such as word processors as ordinary emails.

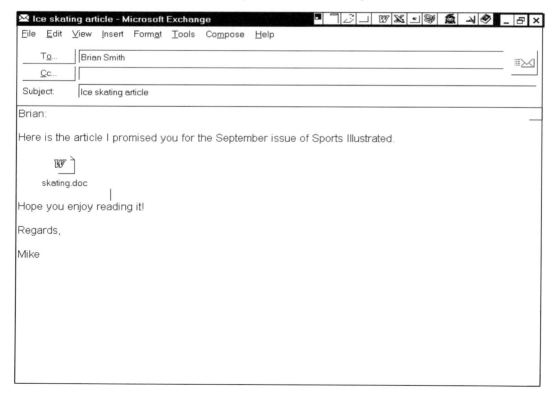

However, the good news is that it *is* possible to send word processing and other files via email. To do so, though, they have to be converted into ASCII format by a special process of encoding. In this form they can be transmitted via the internet as so-called **file attachments**. At the receiver's end they must be decoded and returned to their original form. There are various methods for achieving all this, the most common being UUencoding/decoding, Binhex and MIME.

The above may sound daunting, but from a user's point of view the process is simplicity itself. Most modern email programs convert file attachments to and from ASCII format automatically. Indeed, you will not even be aware that the conversion is happening. However, when sending a message including a file attachment, you do need to check that the recipient has the necessary facility to decode them again!

If you want to send someone a word processing file, this is what to do. The example in figure 3 uses Microsoft Exchange, but similar principles apply whatever the program. Open your email program and create your message in the usual way. Then attach your word processing file by clicking on *Insert* from the menu bar. Select File from the pop-up box which appears, and locate the file you want from the appropriate directory. Click on *OK*, and your file will be inserted into the message.

As you will see, the attachment is represented in your message by a small icon (in other email programs it may be shown differently). The message can now be sent in the usual way. The recipient will see in his/her email program that your message includes an attachment. All being well, he/she will be able to open the file simply by clicking on it.

The pros and cons of email

For writers, email offers many potential advantages:

1. You can correspond quickly and cheaply with fellow writers, even in other countries.

2. You can work with a collaborator, perhaps sending drafts of your work backwards and forwards over the internet.

3. You can email letters and proposals to editors. Most magazines and newspapers are now on the internet.

4. You may be able to submit your finished work via email, thus saving on postage and stationery.

5. And finally, once you have an email address, editors and publishers will have a quick, cheap and simple way of getting in touch with you. The attractions of this from a marketing point of view should be self-evident.

Choosing an email address . . . .

There are a few possible disadavantages, however:

1. Because of the ease of sending email and copying it to other people, you may find yourself receiving a torrent of messages, many of them trivial or unimportant. Email overload is becoming a major problem in many offices.

2. You may become the victim of **spamming**. Spammers are companies or individuals who send out unsolicited advertising messages to all and sundry. You can get software which is meant to filter out spam, but such is the ingenuity of the spammers that some is still very likely to find its way through to you.

Your questions answered

Can I choose my own email address?

Most internet access providers will let you choose your own address, though you will have to use their domain name.

▷ *Example 1* – if your access provider is AOL, your email address will have to end with @aol.com

▷ *Example 2* – if your access provider is Virgin, your email address will have to end with @virgin.net

You can pick any user name you like (subject to certain limits on length/characters), as long as someone else hasn't beaten you to it. If this happens, your access provider will inform you and suggest another name you could use instead. You can accept their suggestion, or try entering another of your own.

How should I begin an email?

There is no objection to starting an email 'Dear Peter'. However, less formal salutations such as 'Hello Peter' or 'Hi Pete' are equally acceptable. Some people simply begin emails with the recipient's name followed by a comma or colon, while other dispense with any salutation and go straight into the message.

How do I know if my email has reached its intended recipient?

With internet email there is no way to be sure. However, if a message cannot be delivered you should receive a message telling you so. This will be sent automatically by a mail server called **Postmaster**. If it is essential to know whether a message has been received, it is a good idea to ask the recipient to confirm via a phone call.

Accessing newsgroups

Newsgroups are, if you like, the next step up after email. A newsgroup is basically an electronic noticeboard devoted to a particular subject.

Anyone accessing a newsgroup can read messages other people have sent in. If they wish, they can then reply to these messages or post other messages of their own.

There are tens of thousands of newsgroups devoted to every subject you can imagine and quite a few you probably can't. The internet network on which newsgroups operate is called **Usenet**. Newsgroups are divided into families, each of which shares a common prefix such as rec or alt. Some of the main prefixes are listed below.

comp	– computer-related groups
misc	– miscellaneous
rec	– recreational
sci	– scientific topics
soc	– social/sociological topics
de	– German-speaking groups
fr	– French-speaking groups
au	– Australian groups
uk	– British groups
alt	– alternative perspectives

So groups which begin rec, such as rec.animals.wildlife, tend to be devoted to hobbies and interests, while those beginning sci, such as sci.astronomy, are devoted to scientific topics. The misc category contains groups which don't fit into any of the other categories, such as the well-known misc.writing.

Probably the most famous/infamous newsgroup family – and still by far the biggest – is that beginning alt. As mentioned, these newsgroups provide an alternative, usually irreverent, perspective on their subject matter. Here are just a few to give you a flavour:

alt.algebra.help (maths homework)
alt.archaeology
alt.astrology
alt.books.roger-zelazny (dedicated to discussing the works of the SF author)
alt.politics.british
alt.tarot
alt.triangle.music
alt.tv.muppets
alt.yoga

Newsgroups are full of enthusiasts who like nothing better than to talk about their pet subject. They're dominated by Americans. And most are **unmoderated** – that means there is no-one in charge to read postings and remove anything unsuitable, provocative or obscene. As a result you can get some frank exchanges of views. While they may not appeal to everyone as a way of passing the time, newsgroups can be useful to writers for research and help in polishing their style. You will find more information about this in Chapters 3 and 4.

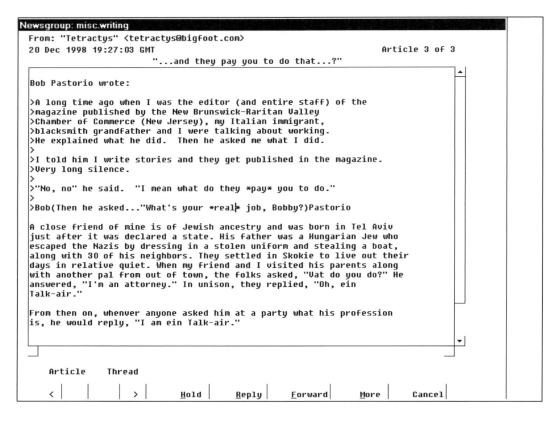

```
Newsgroup: misc.writing
From: "Tetractys" <tetractys@bigfoot.com>
20 Dec 1998 19:27:03 GMT                              Article 3 of 3
                "...and they pay you to do that...?"

Bob Pastorio wrote:

>A long time ago when I was the editor (and entire staff) of the
>magazine published by the New Brunswick-Raritan Valley
>Chamber of Commerce (New Jersey), my Italian immigrant,
>blacksmith grandfather and I were talking about working.
>He explained what he did.  Then he asked me what I did.
>
>I told him I write stories and they get published in the magazine.
>Very long silence.
>
>"No, no" he said.  "I mean what do they *pay* you to do."
>
>Bob(Then he asked..."What's your *real* job, Bobby?")Pastorio

A close friend of mine is of Jewish ancestry and was born in Tel Aviv
just after it was declared a state. His father was a Hungarian Jew who
escaped the Nazis by dressing in a stolen uniform and stealing a boat,
along with 30 of his neighbors. They settled in Skokie to live out their
days in relative quiet. When my friend and I visited his parents along
with another pal from out of town, the folks asked, "Vat do you do?" He
answered, "I'm an attorney." In unison, they replied, "Oh, ein
Talk-air."

From then on, whenever anyone asked him at a party what his profession
is, he would reply, "I am ein Talk-air."


    Article    Thread

    <  |    |    | >  |   Hold  |  Reply  |  Forward  |  More  |  Cancel|
```

Fig. 4 A newsgroup message viewed in CompuServe's CIM newsreader.

How to browse a newsgroup

To access newsgroups you should ideally have a specialist piece of software called a **newsreader** – but nowadays most web browsers will also allow you to explore newsgroups more than adequately. In Netscape Navigator and Microsoft Internet Explorer, the two most popular browsers at present, the procedure is to type

news:

in the Open Location dialog box. You then follow this by typing the name of the newsgroup you wish to visit. For example:

news:misc.writing

All being well, a window will then open with that newsgroup and its messages in it.

Other programs handle newsgroup access differently. In CompuServe, for example, you choose *Go* from the Services menu, type Usenet in the dialog box which appears, and click on *Usenet Newsreader (CIM)*. This will take you to CompuServe's own internet newsreader.

However you get there, once you have accessed a newsgroup, you should see a list of messages (called **postings**), starting from the most recent and working backwards. Some method will also be used to show messages on continuing discussion topics (called **threads**). You can view any message by clicking on the header concerned. A posting from the misc.writing newsgroup viewed in Compuserve's CIM newsreader is shown in Figure 4.

Different browsers and newsreaders present newsgroups in different ways. All, however, will give you the opportunity to subscribe to newsgroups which interest you, read other people's messages, and post messages of your own.

Your questions answered

How can I find out what newsgroups there are?

There are many thousands of newsgroups, with new ones appearing daily and old ones falling by the wayside. There is no single definitive directory of newsgroups, but a useful listing can be found on the world wide web at:

> http://develop.iglobal.net/~dennis/newsgroups.html

How much does it cost to subscribe to a newsgroup?

There is no charge for subscribing to a usenet newsgroup. **Subscribing** simply means that you record (mouse click) an interest in the newsgroup concerned. It will then appear on your list of subscribed newsgroups the next time you log on. You can unsubscribe or resubscribe at any time with a simple mouse click.

I want to access the alt.humour.tasteless newsgroup, but keep getting the message that it's unavailable.

Many IAPs support only a limited range of newsgroups. You may not always be able to gain access to the more obscure or controversial ones.

Is there any other way to explore newsgroups?

You can explore newsgroups on the world wide web via a well known site called DejaNews, at:

> http://www.dejanews.com

DejaNews allows you to browse newsgroups, search for groups with a specific word in their title, read and reply to messages, and post new ones.

Are there any newsgroups about writing?

Certainly! A selection is shown below. Try visiting some to see whether you would find them of use.

```
misc.writing.screenplays
alt.books.reviews
alt.books.technical
alt.censorship
```

Surfing the web ....

Surfing the world wide web

The world wide web (often shortened to the web) is the largest and fastest growing area of the internet. It is also the part which receives by far the greatest publicity. Indeed, new users could be forgiven for thinking that the web *is* the internet.

There are literally millions of documents ('web pages') on the world wide web. Some are simply businesses advertising their wares. Others are run by schools, universities, government institutions, and so on. Quite a few are run by community groups and, of course, by private individuals.

At first glance, a web page looks rather like a Windows help screen with full colour illustrations and text. Web pages can contain much more than this, however. They may include photographs, drawings, sound and video clips, animations and programs. They may also contain interactive features such as order forms you can fill in online and quizzes you can complete and get immediate feedback on.

In addition, web pages have one other very important feature: the so-called **hyperlinks**. These are in effect handy short cuts to other documents on the web. By clicking on a hyperlink you can be transported instantly to another web page, even if it is on a computer on the other side of the world. This makes the web a powerful tool for research.

Understanding web addresses

Every web page has a unique address. This is known as its URL, or **uniform resource locator**. Once you know the URL of a web site, you have all the information you need to visit it. For example, the URL of the Friends of the Earth web site is:

http://www.foe.co.uk

It is worth noting that all web sites begin with the letters http followed by a colon and two forward slashes. When web sites are referred to in the press, therefore, this part of the URL is often omitted as understood, so it would just appear as:

www.foe.co.uk

The remainder of the book will follow this convention.

As previously mentioned, you access web sites by means of a browser. Most IAPs include a browser as part of the suite of programs they provide for new subscribers. The browser is almost always either Internet Explorer or Netscape Navigator. Your browser will automatically install along with the other software.

If you know the URL of a web site you want to visit, select *Open Location* from the file menu and type it in. Be sure to type in URLs carefully, copying all the full stops, colons and forward slashes (and dashes, underscores and tildes [~] where these are included). Avoid putting a full stop at the end of a URL, though it is worth noting that some URLs end with a forward slash. Once you have entered the URL, the browser will try to access the web site for you.

Your questions answered

How do I find out about useful web sites for writers?

Many are mentioned throughout this book, and a wide selection is listed in Chapter 9. You can also read about sites in news-stand magazines such as *Internet* and *.net*. Writing-related web sites are advertised in monthly magazines such as *Writers News* and *Writer's Monthly*.

How about a couple of writing-related web sites to start me off?

Try Pure Fiction:

> www.purefiction.com

and The Eclectic Writer:

> www.eclectics.com/writing/writing.html

As well as useful articles, both of these sites include extensive lists of hyperlinks to other writing sites.

How can I speed up the rate at which web sites load?

One tip is to access the internet in the morning, before the Americans all wake up and log on. Sites with many images take longer to load, so if all you're really interested in is the text, set your browser to text-only.

Using correct netiquette

Netiquette is, of course, the etiquette of the internet. Over the years a mystique has developed around this, but it really means no more than showing consideration for other internet users. The key points of netiquette as it applies to email and newsgroups are listed below:

▷ Keep messages concise and to the point. Don't copy or forward messages to other people unless you are sure they will be interested in them.

Netiquette

▷ Avoid writing in all caps, unless (sparingly) for emphasis. This is known in email jargon as 'shouting'.

▷ Take the trouble to check your grammar, spelling and punctuation. Never believe anyone who tells you that these things don't matter on the internet: they do. This obviously applies with particular force to writers.

▷ Avoid forwarding other people's messages without their knowledge or consent.

▷ Avoid **flaming** (sending abusive messages to people whose views you disagree with).

▷ Don't send unsolicited advertising by email (a much-abominated practice known as spamming).

▷ Don't use jargon, acronyms and so on, unless you are sure the person at the other end will understand them.

▷ Be forgiving of other people's mistakes – remember, we are all beginners at some point.

▷ At the end of a message, as well as your name put your email address. This can be invaluable if the recipient copies your message (for example, to a word processing file) and the header, including your email address, becomes lost.

The internet is a spontaneous, free-and-easy medium, but keep in mind that your messages may one day come back to haunt you. Even if you've deleted all record of your outgoing emails, they are sure to be stored somewhere on someone's computer – possibly those of the recipient, DejaNews, various mail servers on the net, and so on. It is therefore prudent as well as polite to follow the principles of netiquette as set out above.

Abbreviations and emoticons

The internet is characterised by its informality. One aspect of this is the use of certainly widely used abbreviations. Some of the most common are listed below:

BTW	By the way	LOL	Laugh out loud
FWIW	For what it's worth	OIC	Oh I see!
FYI	For your information	OTOH	On the other hand
HTH	Hope this helps	ROFL	Roll on the floor laughing
IAE	In any event	RTFM	Read the flaming manual!
IM(H)O	In my (humble) opinion	TIA	Thanks in advance
IOW	In other words	WRT	With regard to

As well as these abbreviations, in email a whole new language of symbols made up of punctuation marks has evolved. These symbols are known as **smileys** or, more formally, **emoticons**. When viewed on their side, they look a bit like human faces. They are used to show the sender's emotional state – whether he is happy, angry, sad, joking, etc. A huge range of emoticons exists. Some of the better-known ones are listed below.

:-) or :)	happy
:-(or :(	sad
;-)	winking
:-o	surprised
<g>	grin
<G>	big grin
8-)	smile from person wearing specs
:-D	big smile
:-V	shouting
:-#	my lips are sealed

There is of course no obligation to use emoticons, but at least you will now understand them if you see them in other people's messages. Some people find emoticons childish and unnecessary, while others find them an amusing and (possibly) helpful way to lighten their correspondence. They are not normally appropriate in business communications. As with so much on the internet, the final choice is yours.

2 Contacting others

In this chapter you will discover how to:

▶ *find out someone's email address*
▶ *find a designer, illustrator or collaborator*
▶ *send a proposal or a sample chapter*
▶ *join an online writers' circle*

. . . .

Finding someone's email address

Email is a great way of contacting people across the world. An email is quick and convenient to write, and can be sent for the cost of a short local phone call. Before you can email anyone, however, you do of course need their email address.

At the risk of stating the obvious, there is one very simple way of finding out someone's email address: ask them! If you have their phone or fax number, call them up; if you have their home or office address, write to them. If that fails, you will need to do some research.

The bad news is that there is no universal directory of email names and addresses on the internet. However, if you know someone's name and are fairly sure they have an email account, there is a good chance that a little detective work will help you find it.

If you know their internet access provider, you may be able to get their details from that source. Alternatively, try using the free service provided on the Bigfoot web site at www.bigfoot.com. Enter this URL into the Open Location dialog box in your browser. You should see the screen shown in Figure 5.

Bigfoot is a directory listing many thousands of users. Some of the names listed have been obtained from postings to newsgroups, while in other cases users have registered themselves. Let's assume the email address you're looking for is Mark Jennings. Enter that name in the search box, and click on *Search*. After a few moments Bigfoot will come up with a list of people with an email address matching that name. Of course, you may then have to send a few messages to check which of these people is the Mark Jennings you want (Fig. 6).

Bigfoot isn't the only site which can help you trace email addresses. Some other sites to try are:

Four11	www.four11.com
Internet Address Finder	www.iaf.net
WhoWhere	www.whowhere.com
AOL Netfind	www.aol.com/netfind/business.html

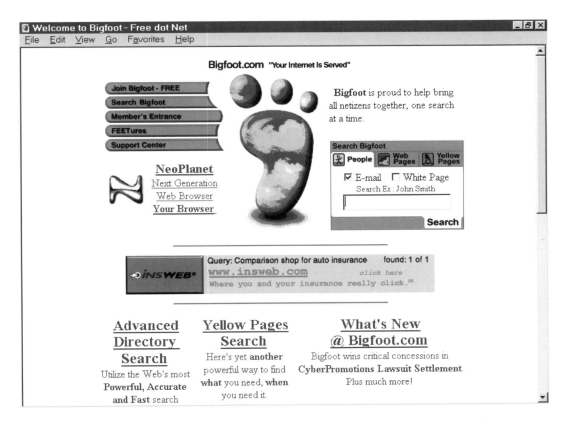

Fig. 5. The Bigfoot home page. You can search white pages and *Yellow Pages* and do an advanced directory search.

Of course, it may be that the person you want isn't registered with any of these directories. In that case there are still some other possibilities:

▷ If you know where they work, check the organisation's web pages. If there is a search facility, enter their name in this.

▷ Enter their name in an internet search engine such as AltaVista at:

www.altavista.com

Hint – set the search engine to look for newsgroup postings, not just web references.

▷ Find out their phone number, then call and ask them. In the United Kingdom, BT Directory Enquiries on 192 is the obvious starting point. For the phone numbers of people living overseas, try the International Telephone Directory web site at:

www.infobel.be/infobel/infobelworld.html

For all the information you could ever want on finding out someone's email address, see the FAQ (Frequently Asked Questions) file on this subject on the web at:

www.qucis.queensu.ca/FAQs/email/finding.html.

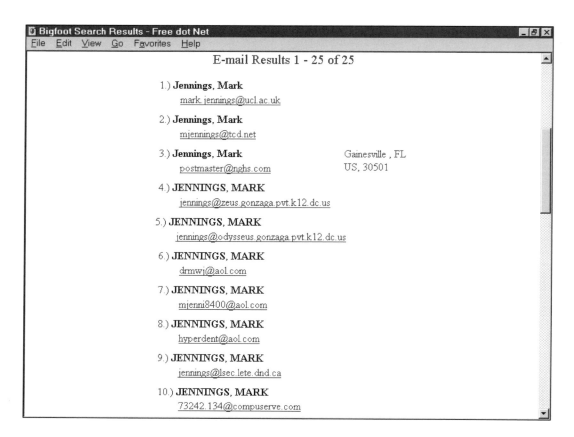

Fig. 6. Example of a Bigfoot results page. In this example it has found 25 results matching the name Mark Jennings.

Finding a designer, illustrator or collaborator

If you need help with a writing project, the internet is the ideal place to start your search. The two most useful resources are newsgroups and the web. For present purposes let's consider designers/illustrators and collaborators separately.

Designers and illustrators

A good way to begin is by placing a message stating your requirements in one of the newsgroups for people working in, or interested in, art and design. For example, if you are looking for an illustrator to collaborate on a children's book, you might post something along the following lines:

'ILLUSTRATOR WANTED. I'm a published writer looking for an illustrator to collaborate with me on a book of modern fairytales for streetwise 8–10 year-olds. I have a letter expressing interest from a major children's publisher. Advance and royalties to be divided 50:50. Please email me privately with details of your experience and background, and we can take it from there.'

Some newsgroups to try for artists and illustrators might include:

> alt.artcom
> alt.art
> alt.arts
> pdx.arts
> rec.arts.fine
> rec.arts.misc
> relcom.arts
> rpi.arts

And for designers, you could try:

> alt.aldus.pagemaker
> alt.cad
> alt.design.graphics
> alt.graphics
> alt.graphics.photoshop
> comp.publish.prepress
> comp.sys.mac.graphics

The above is just a small selection of sites. You can find more by accessing the web site DejaNews (www.dejanews.com) and entering search terms such as 'arts' or 'graphic'. The site will then show you a list of all recent postings to newsgroups which include that term.

There are also web sites which include details of artists and illustrators and examples of their work. One such is the 'virtual gallery' of contemporary fine artists at:

> www.artbeds.org.uk/index.htm

Another very useful resource is Axis at:

> www.lmu.ac.uk/ces/axis/new/whatis/whatis.htm

This is a national register of contemporary British artists. Currently almost 2,500 artists are registered on it.

A final, simple idea is to enter something like 'freelance illustrator' as key words in your favourite search engine. This should produce the home pages of a number of technologically-aware artists and illustrators.

Collaborators

You can find a fellow writer to collaborate on a project by very similar means to those described above. A message to a suitable writing newsgroup is sure to bring a good response, and there are many to choose from. Just a few include:

> misc.writing.screenplays
> alt.books.technical

Sending samples..

alt.journalism
alt.journalism.criticism
alt.usage.english
rec.arts.books
rec.arts.books.children
rec.arts.books.marketplace
rec.arts.poems
rec.arts.prose
rec.mag.fsf.net (fantasy and science fiction)

Of course, you may be looking for a collaborator who is not necessarily another writer but an expert in a particular subject – be it aromatherapy or architecture, astrology or genetics. Again, the easiest way to find someone suitable may be via a newsgroup. Enter the appropriate search term in DejaNews, and see what it comes up with.

A number of web sites and **ezines** (electronic magazines) serve writers. They may be willing to publish your appeal for a collaborator. Try the following:

Poets & Writers Home Page	www.pw.org
Pure Fiction	www.purefiction.com
Bricolage	bricolage.bel-epa.com
Inklings	www.inkspot.com/inklings
Novel Advice Newsletter	www.noveladvice.com

Finally, if you have your own home page (see Chapter 5) you could of course include an appeal for a collaborator on this.

Sending a proposal and sample chapter

The traditional method for selling a book involved sending a synopsis and sample chapter to a number of potential publishers in the hope that one at least might like the idea enough to commission you. The process involved no small expense in terms of postage and stationery. Also there were frequently long waits as your proposal slowly worked its way to the top of the editor's in-tray. That is not to mention the delays caused by the postal service itself. The good news is that the internet has made this whole process a lot faster and simpler.

Most traditional publishers can now be contacted by email, and many have web sites as well. A selection of publishers' web sites can be found in Chapter 9. In addition, a small but growing number of publishers operate entirely on the internet. One example is Online Originals (www.onlineoriginals.com) which distributes book-length works in digital form, using email for both orders and delivery.

Just as with the traditional method described above, it is important to check that your target publisher would be interested in the type of work you wish to offer. For example, there is no point sending a proposal for a gardening book to a publishing house which publishes only fiction. Most publishers' web sites include guidelines for authors and details of their current range of books. Failing this, of course, you can email the publisher asking to be sent a copy of their guidelines.

Netiquette for contacting publishers

Most publishers are happy to receive emailed enquiries. They are busy people, however, so try to avoid sending queries which are easily answered from the publisher's web site or authors' guidelines.

Not all publishers welcome electronic submission of manuscripts, so it is best to send an initial query letter before emailing your full proposal. Even if the publisher asks you to send your proposal and sample chapter through the conventional post, you will at least have introduced yourself, proven your professionalism, and demonstrated that you are clued up about modern technology.

Various web sites and e-zines include submission guidelines from publishers inviting submission of article, story or book ideas. The example below is taken from the electronic newsletter Inklings, available via the web site:

www.inkspot.com/inklings

THE MELIC REVIEW
The Melic Review. 8831 Willowwood Way, Jessup MD 20794. Editor: Jamie Wasserman & al. On-line literary poetry and fiction review. Freq: seasonal. 900 hits/mo. NEEDS: Poetry and short fiction with no limits to size or topic. No genre work please (SF, horror, romance, etc.) With few exceptions, we do not accept previously published material or simultaneous submissions. We ask to be notified if the work has appeared elsewhere. We do not accept material that appears ANY-WHERE else on the web. (Note: this does not include bbs, forums, workshops, &c) PAY: On publication. $5 per poem/essay/story Deadline for the Winter issue is November 27, 1998. RT: 3 mos. TIP: To get a better idea of what we want, read C.E. Chaffin's essay Modulations at http://www.geoci-ties.com/~melicreview/modulation.htm. (ST)
URL: http://www.geocities.com/~melicreview/
GL: http://www.geocities.com/~melicreview/submission.htm
Email: melicreview@geocities.com

This is an example taken pretty much at random. You can find details of more markets in each issue of Inklings, and in some of the other writers' web sites listed in Chapter 9.

Pros and cons of submitting work electronically

Pros

1. You will usually get a quicker response to electronic submissions.

2. There can be considerable savings in postage and stationery.

3. It is as easy to submit work to overseas publishers as it is to those in this country.

4. Using electronic methods demonstrates that you are a go-ahead writer confident about working with new technology.

5. New markets such as online publishers and ezines are opened up.

Cons

1. At present many online publications pay poorly or not at all.

2. Books in which illustrations play an important part (for example children's picture books) may be better submitted in the conventional manner.

3. Not all publishers will accept electronic submissions.

Joining an online writers' circle

If you're looking for contact with fellow writers, not just in this country but around the world, the internet is the number one place to start looking.

Fig. 7. The Lichfield & District Writers home page. The site counter has recorded over 1,000 visits.

To begin with, many 'traditional' writers' groups now have their own web sites. One example is the Lichfield & District Writers (see below).

Lichfield & District Writers' Homepage

Welcome to all aspiring writers living near Lichfield.

We meet on the first and third Thursdays of the month at Lichfield library, the Friary (car park opposite).

We have speakers, manuscript evenings, workshops, a folio and biscuits with your tea/coffee.

Everyone interested in writing poems, short stories, articles, novels etc. is welcome to join us. Non-members are asked to pay £1.50p per meeting (or you could become a member).

Our current programme | About us | Links | Email us

Site visits **1228**

This particular group uses its web site (www.philfr.demon.co.uk/) to provide a range of information. This includes membership details for people who may be interested in joining the group; the current programme of meetings and events; details of the group's annual short story competition; and links to other sites of interest to writers.

The web sites of other groups, such as The Hong Kong Writers' Circle, include additional features such as members' work, announcements and writers' guidelines, classified adverts, and so on:

home.netvigator.com/~lwgray

Links to a number of writers' groups with web sites can be found at the UK-based Pure Fiction web site (www.purefiction.com) and the American site Zuzu's Petals (www.zuzu.com).

Mailing lists

Other writers' groups are entirely internet-based. Often these take the form of mailing lists. An internet mailing list is a way of sending the same email messages to a number of people simultaneously.

Mailing lists can take two forms, open or closed. Closed mailing lists are one-way. They are simply a method used by an organisation to send information to a group of people who are interested in receiving it. That information might concern anything from export opportunities to global weather conditions. An example of a closed mailing list for writers is the Inklings newsletter mentioned earlier.

In open mailing lists, by contrast, the contributions are provided by subscribers themselves. This can lead to some lively debate, though in lists with a core of long-term subscribers in particular, contributions may sometimes wander off the subject. Open mailing lists are the most popular format for online writers' groups.

▷ *Example* – Geoff, an aspiring novelist, lives in a small village in mid-Wales. He feels the need for support and advice on his writing, but doesn't know any other writers or writers' groups. He therefore decides to join a mailing list devoted to fiction writing. Soon he is receiving as many as ten emails a day from other writers across the world. What do you think will be the advantages and disadvantages to Geoff of joining this list?

Examples of open mailing lists for writers include the three mailing lists of the Electric Editors, whose home page is shown in Figure 8.

www.users.zetnet.co.uk/bywater/mail_01.htm

The Electric Editors is a group of UK-based editors with an interest in electronic publishing. They run three mailing lists: Edline, Grapevine and LANGline. Edline provides the opportunity for online discussion of editorial matters, and addresses problems of grammar, punctuation and so on. Grapevine is concerned with computers, and is a discussion forum for people working with computers within the UK publishing industry. The third list, LANGline, is for people working with modern languages, to keep them up to date with current issues and developments. Subscribing to all or any of these lists is free of charge.

Details of over 80,000 mailing lists can be found at the well known Liszt web site at:

www.liszt.com

Liszt includes a searchable database of mailing lists divided into fifteen major categories: arts, business, computers, culture, education, health, humanities, music, nature, news, politics, recreation, religion, science, social.

Fig. 8. Electric Editors home page offers three weekly mailing lists.

The writing section includes eight mailing lists devoted to writing, including a number of workshop-type lists, where subscribers post samples of their work for review by other subscribers. At the time of writing the site includes information on lists devoted to fiction and non-fiction writing, play writing, screen writing, writing by/for young adults, poetry writing and writing by lesbian authors.

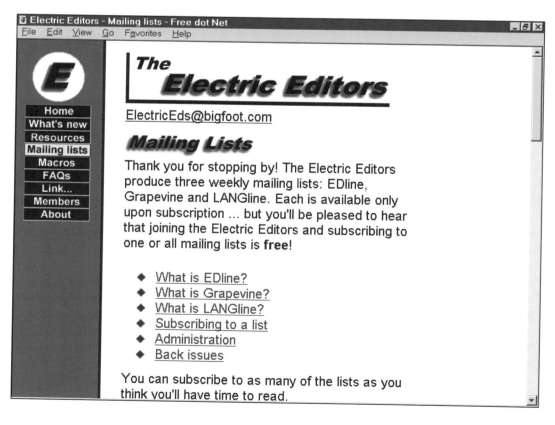

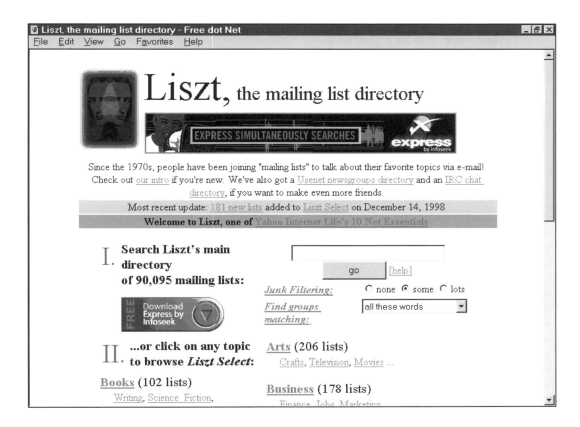

Liszt, the mailing list directory

EXPRESS SIMULTANEOUSLY SEARCHES   express
by infoseek

Since the 1970s, people have been joining "mailing lists" to talk about their favorite topics via e-mail! Check out our intro if you're new. We've also got a Usenet newsgroups directory and an IRC chat directory, if you want to make even more friends.

Most recent update: 181 new lists added to Liszt Select on December 14, 1998

Welcome to Liszt, one of Yahoo Internet Life's 10 Net Essentials

I. **Search Liszt's main directory of 90,095 mailing lists:**

go   [help]

Junk Filtering: ○ none ● some ○ lots

Find groups matching: all these words ▼

FREE Download Express by Infoseek

II. **...or click on any topic to browse *Liszt Select*:**

Arts (206 lists)
Crafts, Television, Movies ...

Books (102 lists)
Writing, Science Fiction,

Business (178 lists)
Finance, Jobs, Marketing

▷ Example – Eve is a professional journalist who has been commissioned to write a series about exotic fruit and vegetables. Through Liszt she discovers a mailing list for people interested in fruit-growing, and sends a message asking to subscribe. When she logs in a few days later, she is disappointed to find only one message via the list which is irrelevant to her assignment. Should she give up on mailing lists and unsubscribe to this one?

Fig. 9. The Liszt home page. This is one of the most popular sources of mailing lists on the internet. The illustration below shows a few of the 200 new lists recently added.

Name	Category	Descripti
1-jobs	Business/Jobs	Job openings in Engin Manufacturing, Oil & Graphic Arts & Printi
2pooches	Nature/Animals/Dogs	A list for everyone wh than one dog!
3threecs	Nature/Animals/Dogs	Scotties, Westies, Cair terriers unite for shari information
3threecs	Nature/Animals/Dogs	Scotties, Westies, Cair terrier cousins unite fo and information
4profit	Internet/Businesss	Dedicated to Online E and How To Market

3 Doing Research

In this chapter you will discover how to:

▶ *use an internet search engine*
▶ *use a directory*
▶ *narrow down a search*
▶ *get help from newsgroups*
▶ *find some top web sites for research*

How to use an internet search engine

For writers the world wide web represents an invaluable source of research information on any subject imaginable. However, finding the information you want from the mass of material out there can be tricky. Indeed, as was noted in the preface, one writer has likened the internet to an enormous library in which someone has turned out all the lights and tipped the index cards over the floor.

It's not entirely needle-in-a-haystack, however. Help is at hand in the form of internet search engines. As the name suggests, these are applications which will help you find sites on the web relevant to the topic you are interested in. They all work slightly differently, but in general you enter a **key word** or phrase in the search engine's dialogue box. You then click on *Search* (or *Find*), and the search engine checks through its records and comes up with a list of sites in which your word (or words) can be found. You can then access these sites directly by clicking on the hyperlinks provided.

Example: AltaVista

One of the best known, and easiest to use, search engines is AltaVista. If you direct your browser at the AltaVista home page, Figure 10 shows what you will see.

www.altavista.com

To illustrate how AltaVista works, let's suppose that you have been commissioned to write an article about Halley's Comet. Having called up the AltaVista home page, enter 'Halley's Comet' in the search dialog box. Click on *Search*, and in a few moments the results will be displayed on your screen.

Figure 11 shows just part of the list provided by AltaVista in response to this query. As you will see, the search results include a brief extract from the text of each of the Web sites. You can access any of these sites immediately by clicking the appropriate link. Once you have found a useful site, you can read it, save the text to disk for later study, or print it out.

Fig. 10. The AltaVista home page. It forms an excellent starting point for searching the internet for all kinds of information.

To use a search engine for the first time, all you need do is enter its URL in the Open dialog box of your browser (after this you can bookmark it or add it to your favourites list). A few of the best-known search engines, with their URLs, are listed below.

AltaVista	www.altavista.com
Excite	www.excite.com
Hotbot	www.hotbot.com
Infoseek	www.infoseek.com
Lycos	www.lycos.com
Open Text Search	www.opentext.com
Webcrawler	www.webcrawler.com

Search engines are powerful tools, and the best news is that most – including all of those listed above – are free for users. They make their profits through advertising.

Pros and cons of search engines

Pros

1. Useful where you have a well defined subject area and need to explore it in more depth.

2. Can produce a range of interesting and useful sites, and suggest avenues of investigation you might not even have thought of.

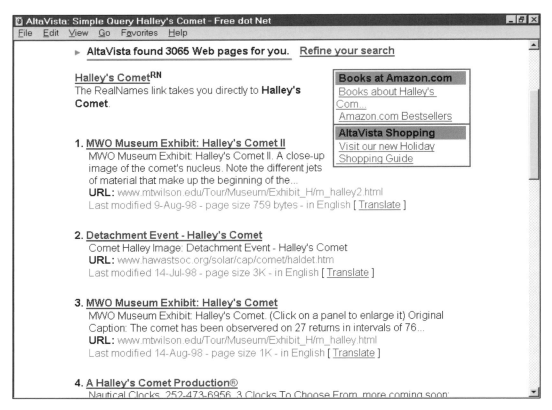

Fig. 11. AltaVista search results for 'Halley's Comet'.

3. Help you narrow down from the many millions of sites on the web those relevant to your particular subject.

Cons

1. Less useful when you have a very specific query, in which case posting a question in a relevant newsgroup may be more productive.

2. Can be time-consuming and frustrating. For example some sites listed may no longer be accessible.

3. Some subjects lend themselves less well to research via a search engine than others.

Examples

1. Freelance journalist Vernon is commissioned to write an article on the subject of cholesterol for a newsletter on health matters. The subject is a new one to him, so he researches it in the conventional way in his local library. Almost as an after-thought, however, he tries entering 'cholesterol' in a couple of his favourite search engines. He is rewarded by several very useful references, including an American 'virtual hospital' site which gives him a large amount of background information.

2. Educational author Frances sees a reference to a psychological concept called the 'Johari Window' and decides she would like to find out more. She tries entering Johari in her usual search engine.

The engine finds just three references to this term. The first is the home page of the Johari Breeding Kennels in Alaska; the second is an article about the tarot written entirely in German (which she doesn't speak); and the third is a promotional site devoted to a US rock group called Johari Window. Frances prepares to give up, but out of curiosity she decides to visit the rock group's site. Lo and behold, she finds a page titled 'How did the band get its name?' Reading this gives her all the information she requires!

How to use an internet directory

At first sight directories appear very similar to search engines, but they work in a different way. A directory is a hierarchically organised collection of web sites. You begin by selecting from a limited number of major categories. You are then presented with a further menu of categories within that category, and keep on selecting from menu after menu until – hopefully – you reach a list of sites relevant to the subject you are researching. This may be best illustrated by an example.

Example of an internet directory – Yahoo!

Perhaps the best-known directory is Yahoo!. This has fourteen top-level categories: Arts and Humanities; Business and the Economy; Computers and the internet; Education; Entertainment; Government; Health; News and Media; Recreation and Sport; Reference; Regional; Science; Social Science; and Society and Culture. See Figure 12.

Let's assume you wish to find out about on-line writing groups. From the fourteen main categories in Yahoo!, the obvious starting point is 'Literature'. Clicking on this brings up another menu, shown in Figure 13. 'Online Forums' looks the most promising category in this list. Clicking on this produces a list of writing groups operating over the

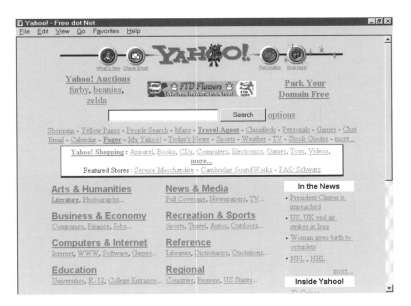

Fig. 12. The Yahoo! home page. Yahoo! is now expanding its services to include special home pages for the UK and other countries. It even has a special vetted area for children, called Yahooligans!.

Yahoo! and other internet directories ....

internet, just as you required. As you will see, Yahoo! gives you a brief description of each web site. Clicking on this will take you to the site concerned.

Other directories

Yahoo! is a popular general purpose directory. In addition, there are many other well-known directories which may be worth trying as well. A selection of the most popular directories is listed below:

Galaxy	www.einet.net/galaxy.html
GOD	www.god.co.uk
Identify	www.identify.com
i-explorer	www.i-explorer.com
Link Centre	www.linkcentre.com
Link Monster	www.linkmonster.com
Magellan	www.mckinley.com
Nerd World	www.nerdworld.com
Search.com	www.search.com
Yellow Pages	www.mcp.com/nrp/wwwyp
Yahoo!	www.yahoo.com

Fig. 13. The Yahoo! 'Literature' menu. Clicking on any of these links will produce a huge number of more detailed and specialised links.

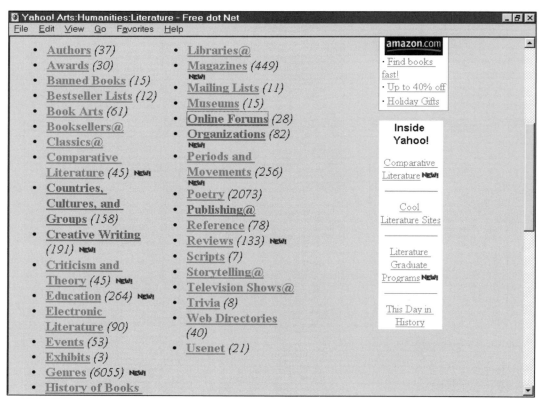

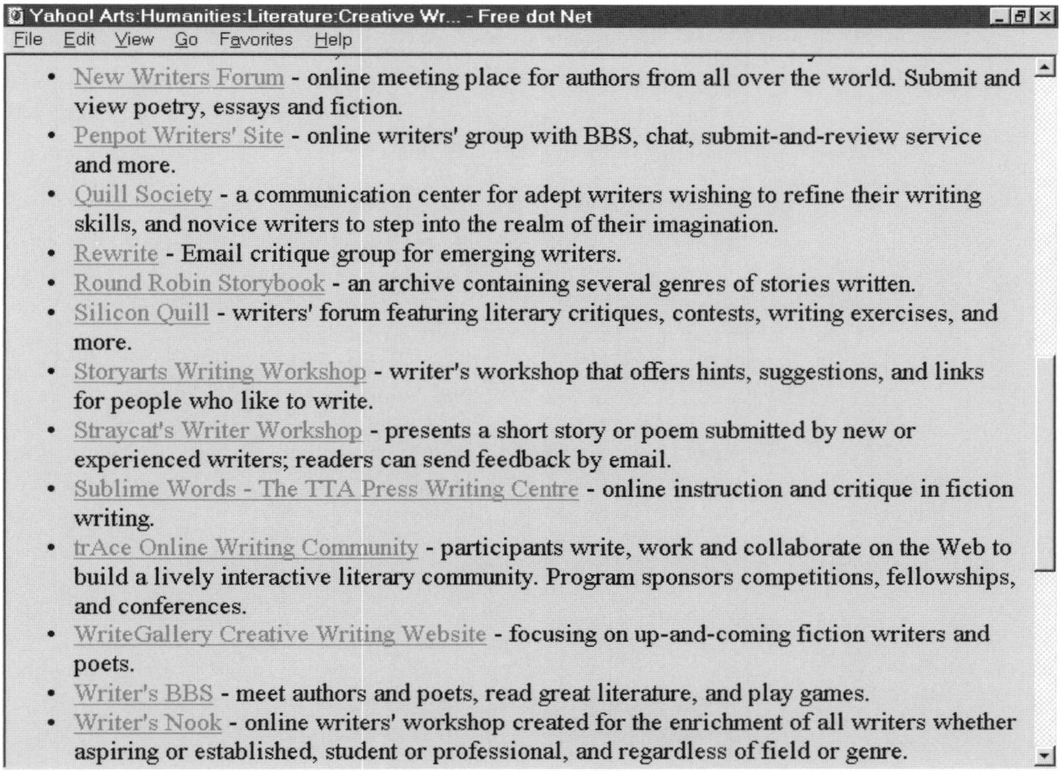

Yahoo! Arts:Humanities:Literature:Creative Wr... - Free dot Net

File   Edit   View   Go   Favorites   Help

- New Writers Forum - online meeting place for authors from all over the world. Submit and view poetry, essays and fiction.
- Penpot Writers' Site - online writers' group with BBS, chat, submit-and-review service and more.
- Quill Society - a communication center for adept writers wishing to refine their writing skills, and novice writers to step into the realm of their imagination.
- Rewrite - Email critique group for emerging writers.
- Round Robin Storybook - an archive containing several genres of stories written.
- Silicon Quill - writers' forum featuring literary critiques, contests, writing exercises, and more.
- Storyarts Writing Workshop - writer's workshop that offers hints, suggestions, and links for people who like to write.
- Straycat's Writer Workshop - presents a short story or poem submitted by new or experienced writers; readers can send feedback by email.
- Sublime Words - The TTA Press Writing Centre - online instruction and critique in fiction writing.
- trAce Online Writing Community - participants write, work and collaborate on the Web to build a lively interactive literary community. Program sponsors competitions, fellowships, and conferences.
- WriteGallery Creative Writing Website - focusing on up-and-coming fiction writers and poets.
- Writer's BBS - meet authors and poets, read great literature, and play games.
- Writer's Nook - online writers' workshop created for the enrichment of all writers whether aspiring or established, student or professional, and regardless of field or genre.

Directories can be helpful when researching a broad-based subject area, especially when that area is difficult to pin down accurately using a key word or phrase. In contrast, they may be less useful than search engines when you have a very specific subject to research. This is illustrated in the case studies below.

Fig. 14. Yahoo!'s listing of online writing groups. The number of such links continues to grow as the internet continues its exponential growth.

Examples

1. Richard is looking for information on the subject of marketing for a business education textbook he is co-writing. Initially he tries entering 'marketing' in a search engine, but all the references which come up are promotional sites for marketing agencies and consultancies. He decides to try the directory Yahoo! instead. Starting within the Education category, he finds a number of useful business education sites on the subject of marketing.

2. For the high-tech spy novel she is writing, Susan needs to find out all about ultra-low-frequency radiation. Initially she tries a directory, but she reaches the bottom levels of the categories for physics and electronics without success. She decides to try a search engine instead. Entering 'ultra-low-frequency' in the AltaVista search engine produces several hundred references for her to follow up.

How to narrow down your search

One problem with doing research using a search engine is that you can still end up with many thousands of sites to investigate. Fortunately,

Narrowing down the search . . . .

there are ways to narrow a search down so that you find only the most useful sites for your purpose. This is done by entering a range of special commands in the search dialog box.

All search engines work slightly differently, but the following terms are in wide general use:

AND

This is the simplest way of narrowing down a search. By entering AND, you stipulate that all sites listed must include both (or all of) your search terms. For example, if you enter 'fruit AND vegetables' in the search box, the search engine will list all sites which include both these words somewhere within them. Sites which contain only one word or the other will be excluded. In most cases, instead of AND you can simply enter a plus sign (+).

OR

By entering OR, you allow the search engine to display any sites which contain one or more of your search terms. Thus, if you enter 'fruit OR vegetables', the search engine will display all sites containing either the word *fruit*, or the word *vegetables*, or both. In place of OR, you can also use a minus sign (–).

NOT

By using the term NOT, you can narrow down your search to sites which include your key word but do not include another specified word. For example, suppose you want information about ducks but wish to exclude any cricketing references (a batsman who is dismissed without scoring is said to be out for a duck). You could enter 'ducks NOT cricket' to ensure that the list of sites displayed excludes any which make reference to cricket.

"MY SEARCH PHRASE"

By putting a phrase in double inverted commas, you can ensure that the search engine seeks out only web sites which include that exact expression. For example, suppose you are researching a feature on the London Marathon. If you simply enter 'London Marathon', most search engines will list all sites including any reference to London and/or any use of the word marathon. By putting the phrase in inverted commas, you ensure that only sites referring specifically to the London Marathon will be found. In some search engines (e.g. AltaVista) joining words with dashes or semi-colons has the same effect as enclosing them in inverted commas.

WILDC*RDS

This is a very useful feature, though unfortunately not all search engines support it. A wildcard is an asterisk which you can place anywhere in your search word or phrase. It will be interpreted by the search engine as any character or none. Wildcards are invaluable if you are not sure how a term is spelt, or you want to cover a number of variations in one search. For example, suppose you need information on the US department store Macy's, but cannot remember whether the name has an 'e' in it or not. If you enter 'Mac*y's', the search engine will find all listings for Macy's and also for Macey's. AltaVista supports wildcards; and other search engines are likely to introduce them soon, if they haven't already by the time you read this.

With the possible exception of wildcards, the above features will work on most search engines you are likely to use. A few more hints and tips on using search engines effectively are listed below.

▷ Make your search terms as specific as possible. For example, if you put 'magic', the search engine will find sites referring to both Paul Daniels-type magic and magic of the mystical variety. In the first instance a better term to use would be 'conjuring', while in the latter it might be 'black magic' or 'occult'.

▷ If you want to find sites where the search term appears either in lower case or with an initial capital, use lower case throughout in your search term. If you want to find only sites containing your search term with an initial capital, use initial caps in the search box.

▷ All the search engines include online advice on narrowing down a search. It is well worth taking a few moments to study the information provided.

▷ You can combine a number of the search commands. For example, you could specify ' "prime ministers" AND Margaret Thatcher NOT Tony Blair' to get a list of all sites referring specifically to Margaret Thatcher's tenure as UK prime minister.

▷ Each search engine is strong in some areas, less so in others. It is a good idea to try a number of different search engines rather than stick to one the whole time.

▷ You may also wish to try a so-called meta-search engine such as Dogpile (www.dogpile.com). This will run your word or phrase through a number of search engines simultaneously and list all the sites they come up with.

How to get help from newsgroups

The world wide web is likely to be your first choice for researching many subjects, but sometimes newsgroups can be more useful. This is most likely to be the case where you have a specific question. Some examples might include:

(a) What is the origin of the expression 'To take a rain check'?

(b) I want to buy a new laser printer. Any recommendations?

Getting answers . . . .

(c) Where can I get a list of all episodes of the TV series *Blake's Seven*?

(d) What is the best way to get into screenwriting?

(e) Can anyone suggest a market for my 80,000 word Regency romance?

(f) Where can I find information on scientific studies of astrology?

(g) I'm planning to visit Jamaica. Can anyone recommend a good, not-too-expensive hotel on the south of the island?

Newsgroups can be a good way of answering questions such as these, as they are populated by people with a specific interest in the topic concerned. For example, the newsgroup

alt.english.usage

might be a good place to seek an answer to the first of the queries above.

Finding the right newsgroup

To use newsgroups for research, your first step will be to identify one or more relevant to your subject area. As previously mentioned, a good starting point is the popular web site DejaNews:

www.dejanews.com

Enter a suitable search term and this site will come up with a list of postings to newsgroups which include your term in the message title.

DejaNews reveals the newsgroup to which each message was posted. In addition, you will see from the headers at the start of messages that many have been posted simultaneously to other groups as well. By making a note of these, you should soon have compiled a list of newsgroups relevant to your area of interest.

Almost all newsgroups have a FAQ (Frequently Asked Questions) list. This is a good place to check what topics the newsgroup covers and any rules or guidelines you should be aware of. As the name suggests, the FAQ includes answers to the questions asked most frequently in the group, so it is a good idea to check that your query has not been answered here already. A list of newsgroup FAQs can be found on the web at:

www.faqs.org/faqs/

Posting your query to a newsgroup

Once you have identified a suitable newsgroup, unless you have an urgent deadline you should **lurk** for a while before asking your question. Lurking may sound slightly dubious, but in newsgroups it is perfectly respectable. It means reading other people's messages without contributing anything yourself.

Lurking will help you get a feel for the group and how it operates – for example, some groups like new subscribers to introduce themselves, while others are not bothered. Lurking will also help you judge the mood of group members and how they would respond to a posting from a writer/researcher. This is an important consideration.

On the plus side, there is a long and honourable tradition among internet-users of sharing knowledge and information. For this reason, most groups will have subscribers queueing up to answer your question. On the other hand, some regular newsgroup members understandably resent people who appear to assume that they are only there to provide them with free answers. Lurking should help you to assess the likely attitude among group members towards your posting.

When you feel confident you have gauged your newsgroup correctly, go ahead and post your query. Be succinct but courteous. Something like the message below should fit the bill.

> TAKE A RAIN CHECK
> I have heard this expression a number of times and am not sure of its meaning or origin. Could anyone enlighten me? Thanks in advance for your help.

It is common courtesy to acknowledge all replies to your query. If the person has left their own email address, you could send them a 'thank you' email rather than clog up the newsgroup with private messages.

Examples

1. *Maddy gets the lowdown on homeopathy.* Maddy has been asked by a publisher to look into the possibility of preparing a self-help book on natural cures for arthritis. She identifies a number of newsgroups concerning arthritis and natural healing, and posts a message asking people to email her with such remedies. When she checks later for messages, Maddy discovers she has a range of replies. One person has sent her several pages of densely written information, while others have sent short descriptions of their favourite cures. She also gets one irate posting from a newsgroup member who resents her using 'his' newsgroup in this way, and details from someone else of an unrelated money-making opportunity.

2. *Vishal goes Dutch.* Vishal is an author of travel books. He is asked to research a book for people planning to relocate to Holland. To do this, he needs information about Dutch housing, employment, schools, leisure activities and so on. He decides to see whether

Reference sites on the internet......................................

there are any newsgroups about Dutch life conducted in English. Via DejaNews he finds a number of newsgroups, and makes an initial posting to each one introducing himself and explaining his project. He receives several welcoming messages with offers to answer any queries he may have, and one person even offers to send him a batch of published information on Dutch life via snail mail (the ordinary postal service).

Top web sites for research

The world wide web is packed with useful reference sites. Of course, search engines and directories will list sites relevant to any particular topic; but for general background research, one of the following sites may provide the ideal starting point.

Encyclopedia.com

www.encyclopedia.com

Fig 15. The Encyclopedia.com home page. This is an example of another site offering masses of free information on the internet.

This invaluable site includes over 17,000 articles from the Concise Columbia Electronic Enyclopedia. There is a search facility, or you can browse through the entire list of articles in alphabetical order. The site also includes links to related web sites, suggestions for further reading, and so on. See Figure 15.

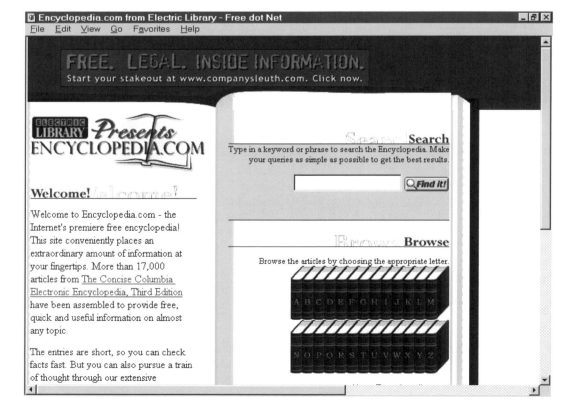

46

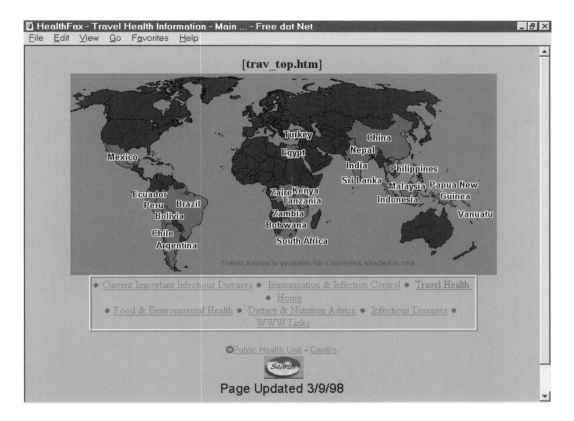

[trav_top.htm]

Turkey

China

Egypt

Nepal

Mexico

India

Philippines

Sri Lanka

Malaysia   Papua New

Ecuador

Zaire   Kenya

Indonesia   Guinea

Peru   Brazil

Tanzania

Bolivia

Zambia

Vanuatu

Chile

Botswana

Argentina

South Africa

Travel Advice is available for Countries shaded in red

● Current Important Infectious Diseases ● Immunisation & Infection Control ● Travel Health
● Home
● Food & Environmental Health ● Dietary & Nutrition Advice ● Infectious Diseases ●
WWW Links

©Public Health Unit - Credits

Search

Page Updated 3/9/98

Healthfax

www.healthfax.org.au/travind.htm

This is an Australian site designed for use by GPs. It covers the whole world, however, giving detailed advice on any special precautions and preventative measures you should take before and during a trip abroad. Consult this site before flying off to an exotic foreign destination on a special commission (or on holiday). See Figure 16.

Project Gutenberg

www.promo.net/pg

This site includes the text of hundreds of books now in the public domain, to be read online or downloaded for later study and analysis. Titles covered include classic novels, poetry and reference works – from Shakespeare to T.S. Eliot, to the Bible. The site is free, but donations are welcome. See Figure 17.

Patient Information Publications

www.patient.co.uk

If you want to find out anything about medicine in the UK, this is the place to start browsing. As well as a range of informative articles, it also includes many links to other sites with detailed medical content. See Figure 18.

Fig. 16. The Healthfax home page. Just click on any of the names on the map to get more information.

Reference sites on the internet ....

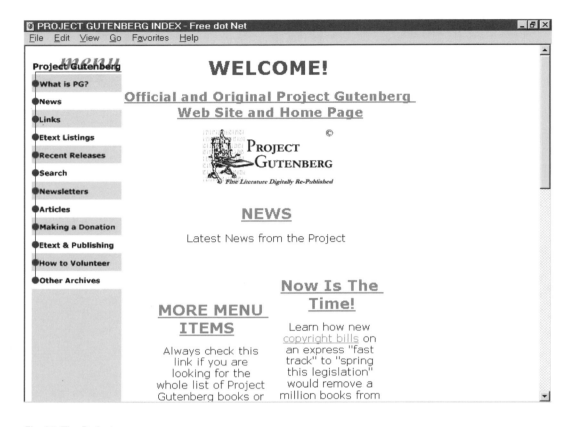

Fig. 17. The Project
Gutenberg home page.

Fig. 18. Patient Information
Publications home page

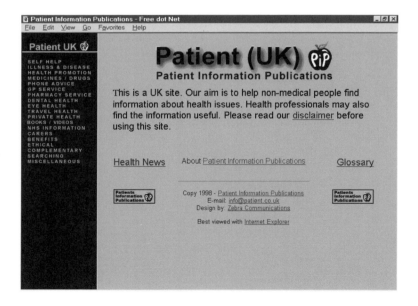

International Movie Database

www.imdb.com

This is deservedly one of the most popular sites on the web. It contains reviews, listings, commercial information and trivia on just about every film ever made. If you need background information on films, actors or the film industry, this is the place to go (it's also great for deciding whether or not the late film on Channel 5 is worth staying up for). See Figure 19.

Fig. 19. IMDB home page.

Fig. 20. The Kitchen Link home page. An essential resource for food writers, The Kitchen Link is an enormous site featuring recipes, health information, news and tips. It also includes links to over 9,000 cookery-related sites. www.kitchenlink.com

4 Polishing your work

In this chapter you will discover how to:

▶ *check your grammar*
▶ *consult an online dictionary/thesaurus*
▶ *get style help from newsgroups*
▶ *have your work appraised*
▶ *enrol on online writing courses*

. . . .

How to check your grammar on the internet

If you want to polish or check your grammar, the internet is an ideal place to start. It is also a good place to get an answer to any grammatical questions which may have been troubling you. Ultimately, of course, many grammatical questions do not have cut-and-dried answers but depend on usage and the opinions of the person you are canvassing. Nevertheless, the internet can help you find out the rules which apply in various situations, and the majority view in less clear-cut cases. There are a number of web sites devoted to grammar, but there are two which are justifiably popular among writers. The first is the Guide to Grammar and Writing:

webster.commnet.edu/HP/pages/darling/grammar.htm

The second is The Slot – A Copy Editor's Guide:

www.theslot.com

Both are North American, so UK readers will have to make allowance for some differences in usage. However, both cover a wide variety of subjects in a readable and informative way.

The Guide to Grammar and Writing

This invaluable site is run by Professor Charles Darling at the Capital Community-Technical College in Hartford, Connecticut, Canada. Detailed information on grammar, spelling and punctuation is provided in three main sections: sentence level, paragraph level and essay level. The essay-level material is relevant mainly to students. Examples of topics you can access at sentence level include:

▷ rules for comma usage
▷ punctuation between two independent clauses
▷ articles and determiners
▷ plurals and possessives
▷ spelling: rules and suggestions

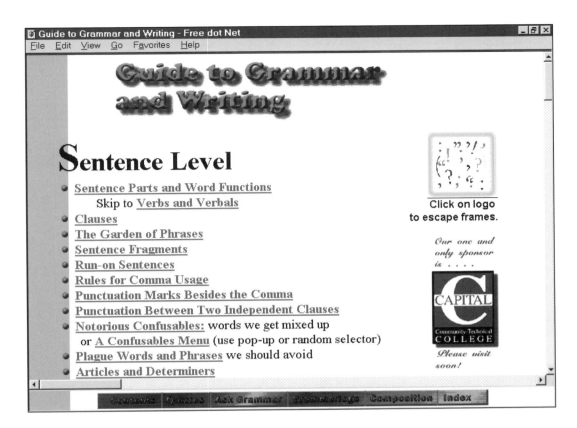

Sentence Level

- **Sentence Parts and Word Functions**
  Skip to **Verbs and Verbals**
- **Clauses**
- **The Garden of Phrases**
- **Sentence Fragments**
- **Run-on Sentences**
- **Rules for Comma Usage**
- **Punctuation Marks Besides the Comma**
- **Punctuation Between Two Independent Clauses**
- **Notorious Confusables:** words we get mixed up
  or **A Confusables Menu** (use pop-up or random selector)
- **Plague Words and Phrases** we should avoid
- **Articles and Determiners**

Topics available at paragraph level include:

▷ sentence variety
▷ consistency of tense and pronoun reference
▷ avoiding primer language
▷ coherence and transitions
▷ paragraph development

You can see any topic by clicking on the relevant item in the main index (shown above). Alternatively you can use the quick-access pop-up menu which is also accessible from the home page.

The Guide to Grammar and Writing also has a couple of other useful features. One is the extensive selection of interactive quizzes. These cover all subjects, from the use of who/whom to finding and repairing sentence fragments. The quizzes are a good way of testing and polishing your grammatical skills.

The second very helpful feature is Ask Grammar. This allows you to submit your own question on any grammatical matter. It is then answered, generally within a day or two, by Professor Darling or one of his colleagues. They do not claim to be the ultimate arbiters where grammar is concerned, but refer to whatever authorities they have used to arrive at their answer. The Ask Grammar service is free of charge and open to anyone anywhere in the world.

Fig. 21. The Grammar and Writing home page. The site provides detailed information on grammar, spelling and punctuation – skills under threat as never before in this age of computers.

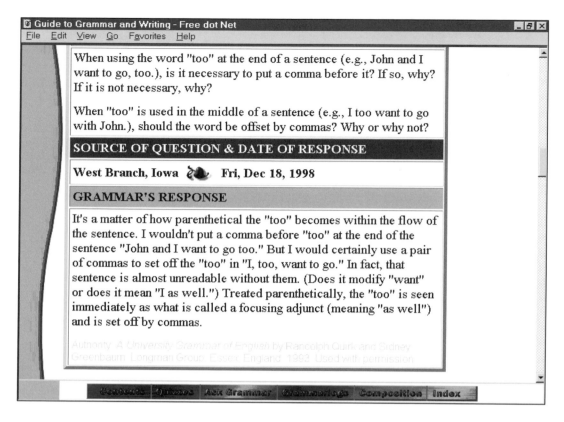

Fig. 22. Ask Grammar Question and Answer.

Answers to Ask Grammar queries are sent direct to the enquirer by email, and are also posted on the 'Grammarlogs' on the site. These form an ever-growing archive of advice and helpful information. There is also a FAQ (Frequently Asked Questions) file of those queries most often raised. If you are not as strong on grammar as you should be (and let's face it, we all have our blind spots), you cannot help but improve through regular visits to this site.

The Slot: a copy editor's guide

While primarily intended for editors, this is another very useful site for writers as well. It is written by *Washington Post* copy editor Bill Walsh. Walsh freely admits to being opinionated – as the self-mocking subtitle 'The Curmudgeon's Style Book' indicates – but the site contains plenty of useful and thought-provoking advice from a man who clearly knows his (American) English.

Various matters are discussed in a large number of short, pithy items. The information is divided into six main sections, as follows:

1. word choice and matters of fact
2. capitalisation, compounds, spelling and style
3. punctuation
4. quotations
5. matters of sensitivity
6. headlines, captions and newspaper issues

You can browse through these categories, or go straight to the topic you are interested in, using the alphabetical index. If you want to know about hyphens, for example, click on H in the alphabetical index (shown below, at the top of the screen). Scroll down until you find the entry for hyphens, then click on that.

Of these two sites, The Guide to Grammar and Writing is probably the more useful on a day-to-day basis, but has a slightly academic bias. The Slot is useful for exploring issues of modern day usage, such as gender bias, referring to people of different races, political correctness, British versus American English, and so on.

Fig. 23. The Slot home page. It includes a section called Sharp Points covering a miscellany of topics from capitalisation to abbreviations and the use of slang.

Your questions answered

Is there an easy way to save information from sites such as these for later study offline?

There are various ways of doing this. One simple method is to highlight the text you are interested in, then copy and paste it into a word processing document. Alternatively, select Save As from the File menu on your browser, and save the material as a plain text file.

I've tried this, but all I got was the index from the left-hand side of the page!

The web site you are visiting probably uses frames. This is likely to be the case if the screen is divided into a number of distinct areas rather like windows. Each frame exists as a separate web page, so you need to be sure you are saving the correct one. The solution is to click within the frame you want to keep before attempting to save the material as a text file.

Dictionaries on line ....

Are there any other useful sites on grammar – especially UK ones?

Certainly – though the two described are among the best. However, we all have our personal preferences, and for grammatical help the following are also worth trying: The Grammar Queen

www.grammarqueen.com

and a UK site, the English Grammar Clinic from the Lydbury English Centre, at:

www.edunet.com/clinic-h.html

To find more, try entering 'English Grammar' in a search engine such as Alta Vista.

How to consult an online dictionary/thesaurus

Most modern word processing programs such as Microsoft Word and WordPerfect do of course include a dictionary and thesaurus. However, dictionary definitions are generally minimal, and the list of alternatives suggested by the thesaurus can be disappointingly short. If you're still lost for words, why not try consulting an on-line dictionary or thesaurus?

Fig. 24. The WWWebster home page.

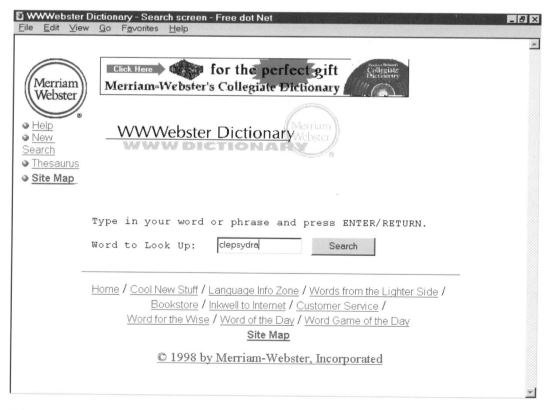

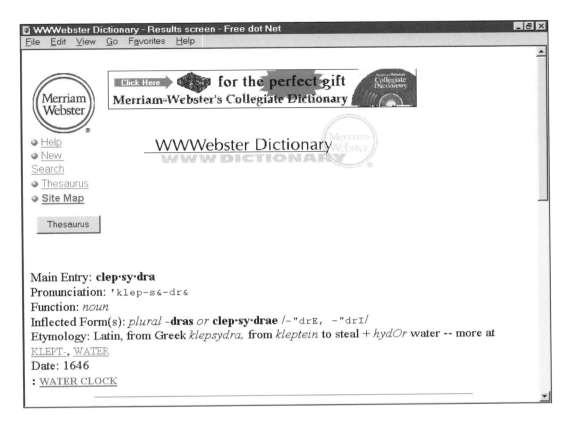

Main Entry: **clep·sy·dra**
Pronunciation: 'klep-s&-dr&
Function: *noun*
Inflected Form(s): *plural* **-dras** *or* **clep·sy·drae** /-"drE, -"drI/
Etymology: Latin, from Greek *klepsydra*, from *kleptein* to steal + *hydOr* water -- more at
KLEPT-, WATER
Date: 1646
: WATER CLOCK

Fig. 25. Example of a
WWWebster definition.

The WWWebster Dictionary

www.m-w.com/netdict.htm
Finding the definition of a word is simplicity itself. In the search dialog box, enter the word you want to look up, and click on the Search button as in Figure 24, and in a moment or two the definition will pop up on your screen, as in Figure 25.

The WWWebster Dictionary also includes a thesaurus and variety of other features, including the Language Information Zone, Word of the Day, and Word Game of the Day.

Research-It!

www.itools.com/research-it/research-it.html.
WWWebster's is a good, general purpose dictionary, but it won't always give you the meanings of the latest terms in science and technology. Neither, in the main, will it provide the meanings of foreign words. Research-It! does all these things and much more.

As well as a Merriam-Webster dictionary, Research-It! includes all the following tools:

▷ computing dictionary (Foldoc)

▷ rhyming dictionary

▷ pronouncing dictionary

▷ thesaurus (Merriam-Webster)

Thesauri on the internet . . . .

▷ universal translator (Logos)

▷ language identifier

▷ anagram finder

▷ English acronym dictionary

▷ biographical dictionary

▷ Bible dictionary

▷ dictionary of quotations (Bartlett)

Research-It! also includes other tools which may be useful to writers, including currency converters, maps, a directory of US phone numbers and so on. This site should be on every writer's list of favourites/bookmarks.

Fig. 26. Research-It! This is an impressively comprehensive and well organised resource – and it's free.

Roget's Thesaurus
humanities.uchicago.edu/forms_unrest/ROGET.html
Both the WWWebster's site and Research-It! include a thesaurus. However, these work in a similar way to the thesauri in word processors: they provide a short list of synonyms for the word in question. On the internet it is now possible to search the original *Roget's Thesaurus* (with 1991 update) by courtesy of the University of Chicago's ARTFL project.

The original *Roget's Thesaurus* had an idiosyncratic structure which arranged all the words in the English language under around 900 main headings with titles such as 'Innocence' and 'Continuance in Action'. While it might not be quite as quick and convenient to use as modern theauri, Roget's version allows users to browse hundreds of words

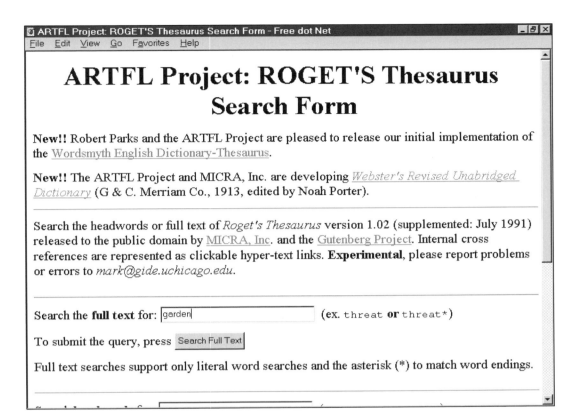

related in meaning to the keyword, rather than just a concise list of synonyms.

Fig. 27. Roget's Thesaurus home page.

You can search for your keyword anywhere in the text or just in the main headings ('headwords'). As an example, let's imagine you want to find some alternative words for 'garden'. Enter this in the first search dialog box, as above, and click on Search Full Text.

The site shows you every category which includes the word 'garden' somewhere within it – giving you enough synonyms to fill a herbaceous border. If you had entered the search term in a second, lower dialog box (not visible in the screen shot), the site would have shown you only those category headings in which 'garden' appears in the main heading.

How to get style help from newsgroups

The web sites mentioned so far can help you with grammar, spelling and punctuation, but such help is not limited to the web alone. Newsgroups are also a valuable source of help when it comes to style.

Newsgroup FAQs

Most newsgroups have their own frequently asked questions files, and those concerned with writing can be a treasure chest of information for writers. For example, here is an extract from the FAQ file for the newsgroup alt.usage.english:

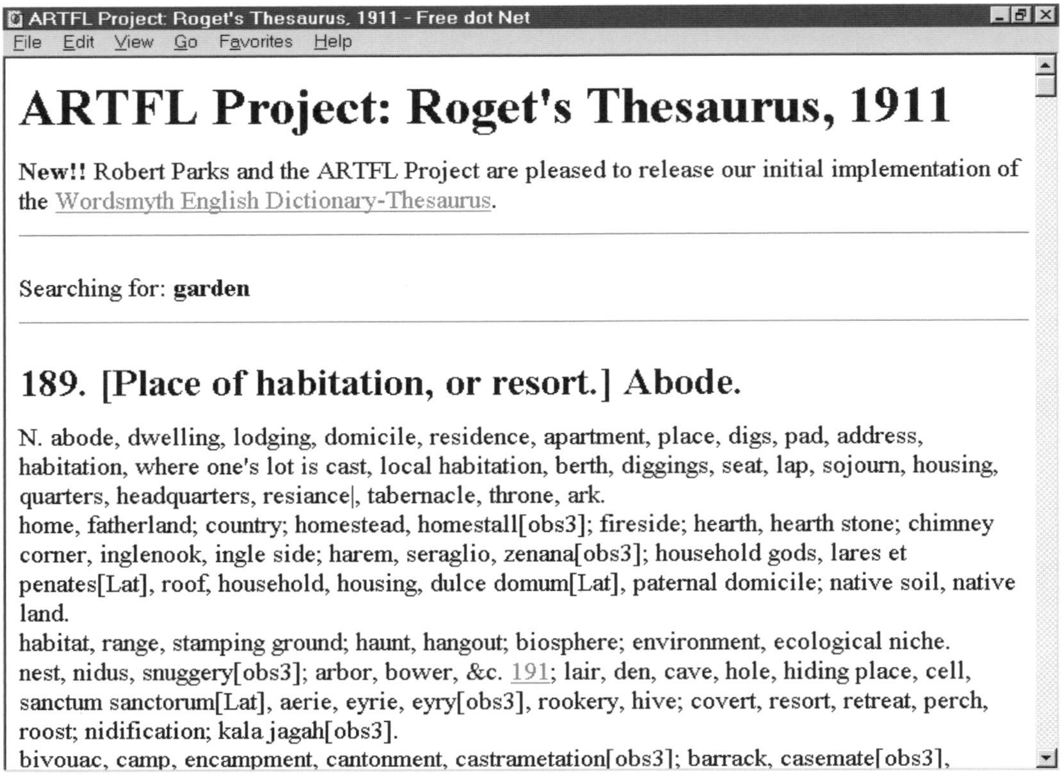
ARTFL Project: Roget's Thesaurus, 1911 - Free dot Net
File Edit View Go Favorites Help

ARTFL Project: Roget's Thesaurus, 1911

New!! Robert Parks and the ARTFL Project are pleased to release our initial implementation of the Wordsmyth English Dictionary-Thesaurus.

Searching for: **garden**

189. [Place of habitation, or resort.] Abode.

N. abode, dwelling, lodging, domicile, residence, apartment, place, digs, pad, address, habitation, where one's lot is cast, local habitation, berth, diggings, seat, lap, sojourn, housing, quarters, headquarters, resiance|, tabernacle, throne, ark.
home, fatherland; country; homestead, homestall[obs3]; fireside; hearth, hearth stone; chimney corner, inglenook, ingle side; harem, seraglio, zenana[obs3]; household gods, lares et penates[Lat], roof, household, housing, dulce domum[Lat], paternal domicile; native soil, native land.
habitat, range, stamping ground; haunt, hangout; biosphere; environment, ecological niche.
nest, nidus, snuggery[obs3]; arbor, bower, &c. 191; lair, den, cave, hole, hiding place, cell, sanctum sanctorum[Lat], aerie, eyrie, eyry[obs3], rookery, hive; covert, resort, retreat, perch, roost; nidification; kala jagah[obs3].
bivouac, camp, encampment, cantonment, castrametation[obs3]; barrack, casemate[obs3],

Fig. 28. Roget's Thesaurus categories list for 'garden'.

"shall" vs "will", "should" vs "would"

The traditional rules for using these (based on the usage of educated Southern Englishmen in the 18th and 19th centuries) are quite intricate, and require some choices ("Should you like to see London?"; "The doctor thought I should die") that are no longer idiomatically reasonable. But if you're dead set on learning them, you can access the relevant section of _The King's English_ at

<http://www.columbia.edu/acis/bartleby/fowler/213.html>.

Usage outside England has always been different, although the historical prevalence of "shall" in the U.S. is sometimes underestimated: Benjamin Franklin said, "We must all hang together, or assuredly we shall all hang separately"; and the Shaker hymn "Simple Gifts" has "To bow and to bend we shan't be ashamed."

The old joke, where the Irishman cries for help: "I will drown and no one shall save me" and the Englishman mistakes this for a suicide resolution, is contrived, in that an Irishman would far more likely say "no one will save me."

Newsgroup FAQs are posted at regular intervals - typically every two to four weeks – to the group concerned. Most FAQs can be found conveniently grouped together in the Usenet Web FAQ Archive at:

www.faqs.org/faqs/

This invaluable site allows you to search for FAQs by newsgroup, category, author, key words, and so on. Writing-related newsgroups with useful FAQ files include

misc.writing

rec.arts.sf.composition
(for science fiction writers)

These can both be accessed via the Oxford University Libraries Automation Service FAQs list at:

www.lib.ox.ac.uk/internet/news/faq/by_category.writing.html

Posting a query

Naturally enough, if you have a query about style or grammar, other newsgroup subscribers will be queueing up to give you the benefit of their wisdom. Here is a typical alt.english.usage query . . .

I'm not sure about the rules concerning where you place the apostrophes in expressions showing possession or association. For example, should it be the children's bedroom or the childrens' bedroom? Also, I've heard it's wrong to use an apostrophe in an expression such as the table's legs. Is this right, and if so why? I'd be very grateful if someone could enlighten me!

And here are a couple of answers received:

The children's bedroom is correct. The way my old English teacher Mr Sanders (God rest his soul) explained this is as follows. First, rephrase the expression using the word 'of'. Thus it becomes 'the bedroom of the children'. The apostrophe must be placed after the last letter of the rephrased version, which of course is the 'n'. As far as I know, this rule is 100% reliable. As regards the table's legs, I don't see any problem with this. The tables legs without an apostrophe would certainly be wrong.

Wrt apostrophes, see the explanation on the Guide to Grammar and Writing (webster.commnet.edu/HP/pages/darling/grammar.htm). 'The table's legs' is wrong because an inanimate object like a table cannot by definition possess anything. You should always write 'the legs of the table', or find some other way round it. HTH.

Appraisal services ....

It is worth noting that not everyone who subscribes to a newsgroup will be an expert by any means. As with so much on the internet, you will have to judge for yourself how reliable is the information you are given. If in doubt, write back to the person thanking them for their response, and asking if they can give you any published or online references to back up their assertion.

Getting your work appraised

An increasing number of internet-based services now offer to give appraisals of writers' work. As with traditional appraisal services you will be expected to pay a fee for an expert opinion, but on-line appraisal does offer a number of distinct advantages:

▷ Delays due to the postal service are eliminated.

▷ There are savings on postage and stationery.

▷ Online work for appraisal can easily be sent to more than one appraiser at the same time.

There are some disadvantages, however:

▷ Layout and formatting (for example italics) can become lost or distorted in email.

▷ There may be problems of compatibility between the appraiser's and the client's machine.

▷ Appending comments to an emailed script is not as straight-forward as the traditional red pen on paper.

Lifelines

Lifelines is an email based service run by professional freelance writer Joanna Parfitt. It is part correspondence course, part writers' circle and part appraisal service.

For a £35 fee, members receive twelve monthly tutorials which end with a task which they are asked to return by the end of the month. Members can have up to four pieces of work a year appraised by Joanna, and the work is sent to other people enrolled in Lifelines for their comments as well. You can send work completed in fulfilment of one of the monthly tasks, or something else. If you want more than four pieces of work appraised in a year, you will have to pay an additional fee.

Lifelines' members get constructive criticism from Joanna and other members, and also receive advice and ideas on marketing their work. Any separate queries are answered for no extra charge. Some other benefits of membership include:

▷ You receive the email addresses of other members, so that you can start your own email friendships with fellow writers.

▷ A web site is planned (and may be on-line by the time you read this) where the best work will be published.

▷ Joanna Parfitt runs Summertime Publishing, which endeavours to publish new talents when possible.

More information about Lifelines can be obtained by sending an email request to:

summertime@lineone.net

The Inner Circle Writers Club

This is a free club for fiction writers from around the world. Through the club you can share writing tips and techniques, check your research with people who know first-hand, and exchange manuscripts for critiques. The group has around 1,500 members, many of whom enjoy appraising other members' work. Of course, you have no guarantees concerning the credentials or publishing record of the person doing the appraising!

If you wish to join The Inner Circle, you have to fill in a questionnaire on their web home page at:

www.geocities.com/circlefaq.htm

The information you provide is then placed online on the club's profile pages, accessible to members only. Using the membership list, you will be able to find many writers of similar age, writing interests, and reading preferences as your own. It is then open to you to write to these members asking them if they will appraise your work (and they, of course, can ask you to do likewise).

Members of the Inner Circle Writers Club receive a range of other benefits, including the club's fortnightly newsletter QWERTY. If you wish to have your fiction appraised free of charge by other writers, and don't mind too much that most will have limited publishing experience, then joining the Inner Circle Writers Club could be a very worthwhile step.

How to enrol on an online writers' course

Writing courses using the internet are becoming commonplace. Most of the traditional, mail-based correspondence colleges are at least willing to accept students' work submitted in the form of email.

The UK's largest correspondence school for writers is the Manchester-based Writers Bureau (see Figure 29). Director of Studies Diana Nadin says: 'We have no plans to put our actual course material on the net – we can't see any advantage in that for ourselves or our students. But if students want to send assignments by email, that's fine. When they enrol we send them a questionnaire asking about their computer and

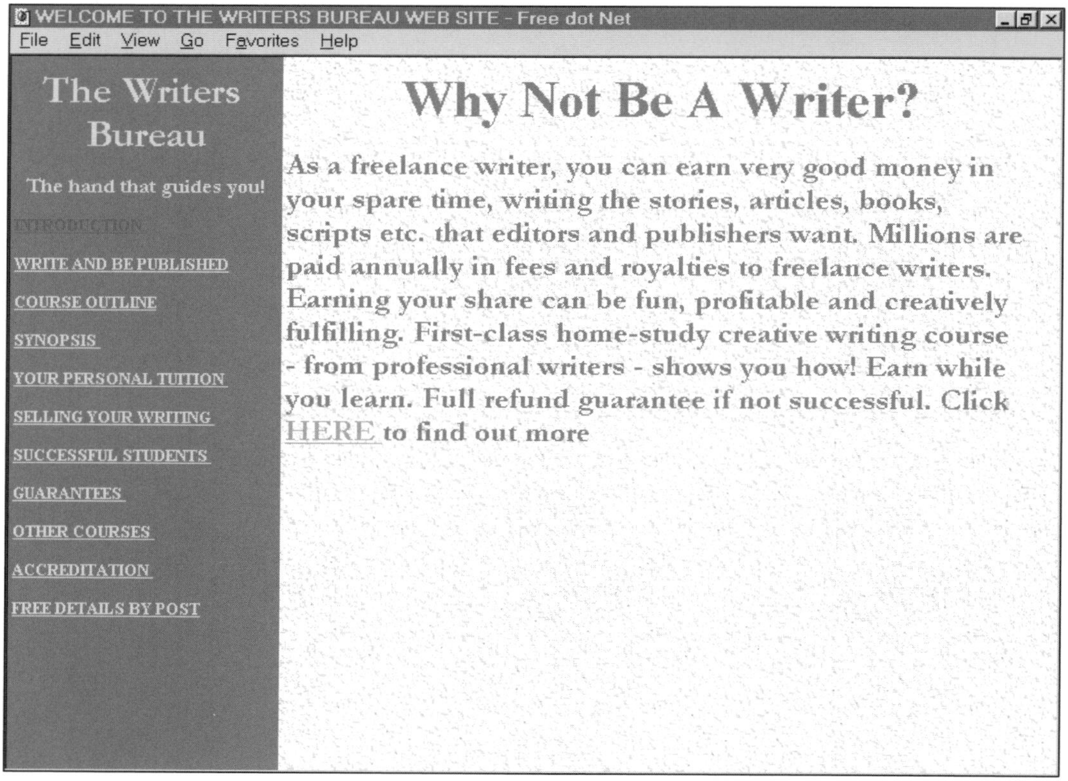
WELCOME TO THE WRITERS BUREAU WEB SITE - Free dot Net
File Edit View Go Favorites Help
The Writers Bureau
The hand that guides you!
INTRODUCTION
WRITE AND BE PUBLISHED
COURSE OUTLINE
SYNOPSIS
YOUR PERSONAL TUITION
SELLING YOUR WRITING
SUCCESSFUL STUDENTS
GUARANTEES
OTHER COURSES
ACCREDITATION
FREE DETAILS BY POST
Why Not Be A Writer?
As a freelance writer, you can earn very good money in your spare time, writing the stories, articles, books, scripts etc. that editors and publishers want. Millions are paid annually in fees and royalties to freelance writers. Earning your share can be fun, profitable and creatively fulfilling. First-class home-study creative writing course - from professional writers - shows you how! Earn while you learn. Full refund guarantee if not successful. Click HERE to find out more

Fig. 29. The Writers Bureau home page.

email program, and we make sure they're assigned to a tutor who has a compatible set-up.' Mrs Nadin says that they are happy to receive enquiries by email at:

writersbureau@zen.co.uk

The Writers Bureau also has a web site at:

www.writersbureau.com

Another of the 'traditional' writing schools, the Australian-based Morris School of Journalism, also has a web site:

www.morriscollege.com.au/

and accepts email assignments and enquiries:

westonj@morriscollege.com.au

Courses on offer from the Morris School include:

▷ Professional Freelance Journalism

▷ Professional Freelance Photography

▷ Freelance Cartooning & Illustration

▷ Freelance Entertainment Writing & Photography

▷ Freelance Travel Writing & Photography

▷ Freelance Sports Writing & Photography

▷ Professional Children's Writing

▷ Professional Crime & Suspense Writing

▷ Professional Romance Writing

▷ Professional Script Writing

▷ Public Relations, Publicity & Promotions

Web-based writing courses

Other writing courses are available entirely over the web. An example is the range of courses on offer at The Friendly Pencil:

www.writelinks.com/fp/

In Friendly Pencil courses you work one-on-one with the instructor at your own pace. Lessons are conducted by email, with course material available on the web. Two of the most popular courses are 'The Nuts and Bolts of Fiction Writing' and 'Poetry Basics'.

Fig. 30. The Friendly Pencil home page. The Friendly Pencil is a US-based service run by three professional writers, Janet Kent, Deck Deckert and Mariska Stamenkovic.

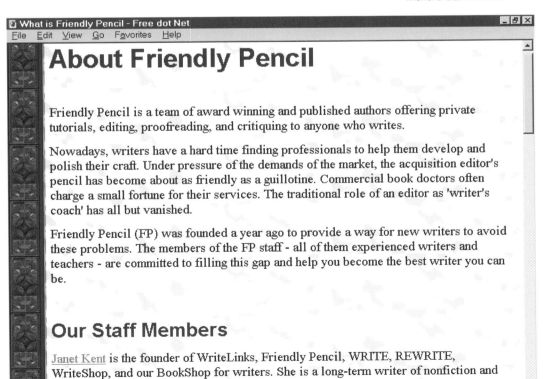

What is Friendly Pencil - Free dot Net

File Edit View Go Favorites Help

About Friendly Pencil

Friendly Pencil is a team of award winning and published authors offering private tutorials, editing, proofreading, and critiquing to anyone who writes.

Nowadays, writers have a hard time finding professionals to help them develop and polish their craft. Under pressure of the demands of the market, the acquisition editor's pencil has become about as friendly as a guillotine. Commercial book doctors often charge a small fortune for their services. The traditional role of an editor as 'writer's coach' has all but vanished.

Friendly Pencil (FP) was founded a year ago to provide a way for new writers to avoid these problems. The members of the FP staff - all of them experienced writers and teachers - are committed to filling this gap and help you become the best writer you can be.

Our Staff Members

Janet Kent is the founder of WriteLinks, Friendly Pencil, WRITE, REWRITE, WriteShop, and our BookShop for writers. She is a long-term writer of nonfiction and fiction and experienced leader of writers' workshops.

Web-based seminars

The five main 'seminars' of the fiction-writing course are shown below:

▷ Stuff Happening: The Elements of Drama

▷ Beginning, Middle and End: The Basic Structure of Fiction

▷ Whose Story Is This Anyway? Point of View

▷ Contrast, Conflict and Confrontation: The Story's Engine in Close-up

▷ It's Alive! How to Write Powerful, Vivid Prose

Each seminar focuses on one aspect of fiction and explores the techniques involved through examples and assignments. Seminars comprise four to six lessons, taken at weekly intervals. You can take as much time as you need between seminars, but they cannot be taken out of sequence.

You can see the course material for the fiction-writing course free of charge on the web page:

www.writelinks.com/fp/tutorials.html

In addition to the courses mentioned here, others are also available by arrangement.

Marketing Your Business on the Internet

A practical step-by-step guide for all business owners and managers

Sara Edlington

Is your business online? Or perhaps you are still wondering whether to take the plunge? Written by someone experienced in marketing on the internet from its earliest days, this practical book will show you step-by-step how to make a success of marketing yourself and your organisation on the internet.

- User-friendly – very easy for the marketing user to understand
- Illustrated – with lots of clear examples and typical web sites
- Comprehensive – a complete practical introduction
- Authoritative – written by an experienced internet trainer
- Value-for-money – to help you get the most out of the internet

Sara Edlington is editor of *Marketing Communications Update*. She has written widely on internet and communications topics for *The Times*, *The Independent*, *Internet Today*, *Marketing* and many other journals.

Internet Handbooks Series – Send for free catalogues
£16.99 paperback. 246 x 170mm. ISBN: 1 84025 304 5
Plymbridge Distributors Ltd, Estover Road, Plymouth PL6 7PY, UK.
Customer Services tel: (01752) 202301. Orders fax: (01752) 202331

5 Marketing yourself online

In this chapter you will discover how to:

▶ *publish your writing on the net*
▶ *find jobs and assignments*
▶ *promote yourself and your work*
▶ *set up your writer's home page*

. . . .

How to publish your writing on the net

There are various places you can publish your writing on the net. Some of these are fee-paying, while others simply provide the opportunity of a 'shop window' for your writing skills.

Online Originals
www.onlineoriginals.com.
Online Originals is a publishing company operating entirely on the internet. It distributes book-length works in digital form, using email for both orders and delivery. Online Originals publishes fiction, non-fiction and drama (see Figure 31).

Fig. 31. Online Originals' home page.

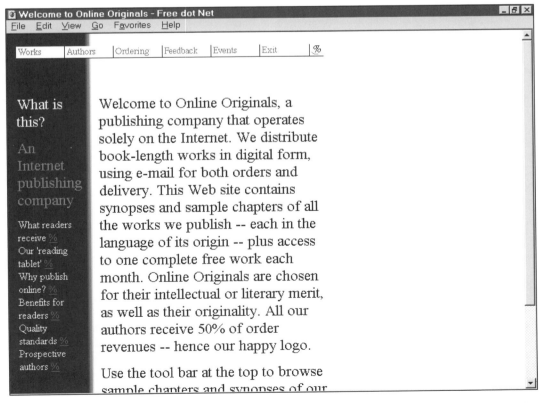

> **Welcome to Online Originals - Free dot Net**
> File Edit View Go Favorites Help
>
> | Works | Authors | Ordering | Feedback | Events | Exit | % |
>
> **What is this?**
>
> An Internet publishing company
>
> What readers receive %
> Our 'reading tablet' %
> Why publish online? %
> Benefits for readers %
> Quality standards %
> Prospective authors %
>
> Welcome to Online Originals, a publishing company that operates solely on the Internet. We distribute book-length works in digital form, using e-mail for both orders and delivery. This Web site contains synopses and sample chapters of all the works we publish -- each in the language of its origin -- plus access to one complete free work each month. Online Originals are chosen for their intellectual or literary merit, as well as their originality. All our authors receive 50% of order revenues -- hence our happy logo.
>
> Use the tool bar at the top to browse sample chapters and synopses of our

Managing Editor David Gettman says: 'There is no cost to the author in publishing a work with Online Originals; we pay the authors royalties of 50%. When we receive a submission it goes by email to our professional readers – who specialise in fiction, non-fiction or drama – based here in Europe. We respond with specific comments and a 'yes' or 'no', usually in weeks, not months. If we say 'yes' we send a letter and contract by conventional mail.' Readers can see an extract of each work on the web site. If they wish they can then pay a fee to receive the entire text. You can obtain submission guidelines by emailing a request to:

editor@onlineoriginals.com

Hafod Publishing
www.hafod.demon.co.uk
Hafod Publishing is run from their home in Wales by Celia and Duncan Adams. They are looking for unpublished novels to market via their web site. They say that they that as long as your book is well written, well plotted and contains no illegal or libellous content, they will probably be prepared to publish it on their site.

Books available from Hafod Publishing are categorised by genre, ranging from adventure to mystery, whodunnits to science fiction, children's novels to westerns. As with Online Originals, potential

32. Hafod Publishing home page

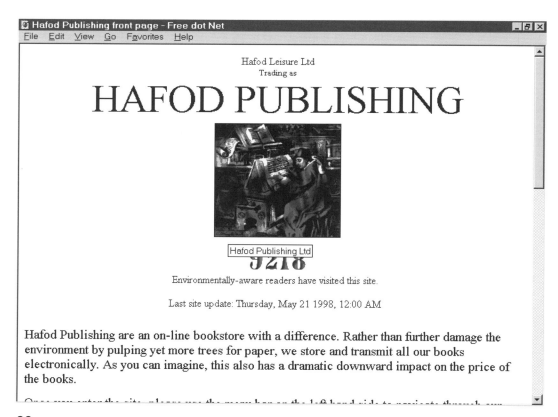

Hafod Publishing front page - Free dot Net

File   Edit   View   Go   Favorites   Help

Hafod Leisure Ltd
Trading as

HAFOD PUBLISHING

Hafod Publishing Ltd
ひとつ

Environmentally-aware readers have visited this site.

Last site update: Thursday, May 21 1998, 12:00 AM

Hafod Publishing are an on-line bookstore with a difference. Rather than further damage the environment by pulping yet more trees for paper, we store and transmit all our books electronically. As you can imagine, this also has a dramatic downward impact on the price of the books.

buyers can see an extract from each title free of charge. They can then pay a fee to receive the entire text by email.

Books are priced at about half the amount which would be charged if they were in the form of paperbacks. Royalties are paid at 20% of the sale price. Authors retain all rights except internet rights.

Hafod also accepts books which have been published in conventional form. This could provide a means of getting extra exposure (and sales) for existing titles. Hafod say they will agree terms for selling the electronic version of your book with the publisher concerned.

The Poetry Exchange
www.w3px.com
As the name suggests, this is a site where poets can have their poems published free of charge. Based in Hertfordshire, England, it is run by Chris Curtiss, a staff member of the University of Oregon. The aims of the Poetry Exchange are:

▷ To provide a medium for poets to publish their works on the world wide web.

▷ To encourage as many individuals and organisations as possible to access and use the Poetry Exchange.

▷ To become a resource centre for help, guidance, software and all things connected with poems and poetry.

▷ To help poets experiment with the unique opportunities offered by the evolving medium of the world wide web.

▷ To be equally accessible to novice and skilled, young and old.

Anybody, anywhere can submit poems to the Poetry Exchange using the submission form on the web site. English or any other language is accepted. Poems appear on the site within a couple of days.

Pros and cons of publishing on the internet

Pros
1. Your work can reach a huge, world wide audience.

2. Publication is much faster – usually a few weeks at most.

3. You save on postage and stationery when submitting.

4. You can still sell other, non-Internet rights in your book.

Cons
1. There is no guarantee that anyone will visit the site.

2. The work may no longer qualify as 'unpublished' for competitions, etc.

3. Your work is unlikely to be professionally edited and proofread.

4. Downloading an email is not as convenient as opening a book – will readers be prepared to pay to obtain your script in this form?

How to find writing jobs and assignments

More and more organisations are advertising for writers on the internet. The majority are in North America, but there is also a growing number of UK and other publishers and agencies using the net to seek writers.

And, of course, there is nothing to stop writers outside America applying for jobs and commissions there. With the internet, it is as simple to work for a client in another continent as it might be for one in the next street.

Using a search engine

A simple, but effective, starting point is to enter 'writers wanted' in your favourite search engine. For example, Lycos (www.lycos.com) came up with the following promising-looking sites, among others:

Aci Plus
www.aci-plus-com/jobdesc1.htm
An American company seeking full-time professional writers to produce 'model essays' on various subjects for English students across the world.

American Education Systems
www.aespub.com/writers
This is a small, independent company publishing correspondence courses, books and articles. The topics they cover range from insurance to business development, marine education to gardening and landscaping. Forthcoming projects include a consumer tip series and articles on alternative medicine and healthcare. Non-fiction writers are invited to submit a query letter and outline.

Writers Bureau
www.personal.u-net.com/~bureau/home.htm
A British agency seeking freelance writers with a scientific (preferably medical/pharmaceutical) background.

SP research
paperspapers.com
An American company looking for full- or part-time writers to produce model research papers. Writers must have a degree, a wide range of knowledge, and the ability to write quickly to a prescribed style.

Trippin' Out
www.trippinout.com/writers.html
The web site of Trippin' Out magazine, an American alternative travel

magazine; they are looking for writers who are 'really familiar with a hip destination'.

Of course, by the time you read this book these vacancies may have been filled and the sites themselves have disappeared. However, others will undoubtedly have sprung up in their place.

Sites with commissions, jobs and grants for writers

There are also a number of sites which publish information on commissions, full- and part-time jobs, and grants available for writers. Some of these are listed below, with a further selection in Chapter 9.

Authorlink
www.authorlink.com
Authorlink is a highly professional American site claiming more than 125,000 readers a year. It is packed with news of the US publishing industry, and includes plenty of market information. You can also submit your unpublished book or manuscript for possible showcasing on the site.

Inklings
www.inkspot.com/inklings
The electronic newsletter Inklings was mentioned in an earlier chapter, but as a great source of up-to-date market information it can hardly be omitted here. Each fortnightly issue of Inklings is emailed free to subscribers, and includes information on a range of paying markets for freelance writers.

Market List
www.marketlist.com
The Market List is a free resource for writers of science fiction, fantasy and horror. It includes articles, reviews, interviews and market information for writers in these genres. Links to other relevant sites and earlier, archived versions of the list are provided.

Mystery Opportunities
www.slip.net/~cluelass/Opportunity.html
As the name suggests, this site publishes market information of interest to mystery writers, from beginners to published professionals. There are details of awards and competitions, calls for submissions, and advertisements from publishers requiring writers.

Poets and Writers Home Page
www.pw.org
As well as feature articles, this American site includes an extensive classified advertising section. Calls for manuscripts are set out in four main categories: anthologies, books, chapbooks (small poetry and fiction books) and magazines. There are also sections for conferences, contests, full-time jobs, publications, rentals/retreats, services, work-shops and internet sites.

Newsgroups for writers..

Writers Guild of Great Britain
www.writers.org.uk/guild
The Writers Guild of Great Britain's site has classified advertisements for a range of market opportunities including, at the time of writing, invitations to submit film, TV and play scripts.

Writers Write
writerswrite.com
Writers Write is another information-packed resource for writers. It includes detailed guidelines for online and printed publications requiring fiction, humour, plays, poetry and screenplays. There is also a list of paying markets, including calls for submissions from publishers and agents.

Newsgroups

Finally, it is well worth monitoring newsgroups such as:

misc.writing

rec.arts.prose

as requests for submissions are regularly posted here. It must be said, however, that many postings are for small magazines paying in complimentary copies or token fees. The following posting from the misc.writing newsgroup is typical:

New Market!

Hidden Manna is a new literary journal concerned with the role of story in faith. We celebrate paradox in Christian and Jewish faith, stories that make riddle out of answer. We are now accepting fiction, essays, interviews, and poetry. During 1999 will pay in copies and subscription, increasing to cash payments in year to follow. Most subscribers receive hard copy journal, but we also distribute via email attached files.

Guidelines are available at
http://members.tripod.com/~hiddenmanna/index.html

Email queries or full manuscripts to hiddenmanna@triquetra.org

Your questions answered

How can I limit my 'writers wanted' search to British and Irish sites?

Many search engines (Lycos and Hotbot are two examples) will allow you to limit a search to a particular country or countries. Alternatively, you can add the words AND UK to your search term to ensure that all the sites listed have the word UK somewhere within them.

*Can a writer based in the UK or Europe really get work in the USA
via the internet?*
Certainly! However, it is a good idea to avoid drawing attention to your
non-American status needlessly. If asked your fees, for example,
quote them in US dollars. It can also be beneficial to have an email
address which does not identify you as non-American, by using AOL or
Compuserve, for example. If you have an email address which is
clearly UK-based, get a free, web-based email account such as Hotmail
(at its US site, www.hotmail.com) and use that for contacting
American editors.

*Are all jobs and opportunities advertised on the internet equally
suitable for non-US writers?*
Probably not. This is really a matter of common sense and marketing
yourself and your work appropriately. With fiction, in theory your home
country should make no difference. For some areas of non-fiction (e.g.
baseball, restaurant reviews, US politics) living outside the USA is
likely to be a handicap. Then again, you can always use your non-
American status to propose articles with a fresh, different perspective.
Many topics that would seem routine in Britain or Europe may appear
new and exotic to an American audience.

How to promote yourself and your work

As any professional writer knows, when it comes to selling your
services, replying to advertisements is only half the story. You must
also advertise yourself and your work to potential clients. The internet
offers a number of promising, low-cost ways of doing just that.

There are a number of sites where writers can post their details and/or
examples of their work. One such is Authorlink!, mentioned earlier in
this chapter (see Figure 33).

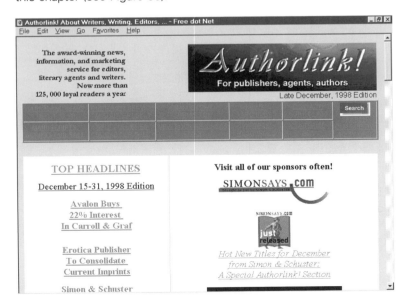

Fig. 33. Authorlink!
home page

Online showcasing ....

Authorlink
www.authorlink.com
You can submit full-length manuscripts (fiction or non-fiction) for possible inclusion in the Author Showcase section of Authorlink! The people behind Authorlink! claim to be extremely successful in matching writers with literary agencies in this way. They say that 65 to 75% of their evaluated manuscripts are requested by agents and editors. Of these, they say 30 to 36% percent are accepted for literary representation.

All submissions for Author Showcase are reviewed by a committee of published writers. There is no reading fee. If successful, your listing will appear in Author Showcase for experienced writers. Those not chosen for Author Showcase but who demonstrate good potential are listed in the Emerging Writers section for developing talent. Even if a work is rejected it may be submitted a second time after editing. Submissions of new work are always welcome.

Authorlink does not put the entire typescript of a book on the internet, but a synopsis and sample with author details. When interest is expressed by an editor or agent, Authorlink! immediately notifies the writer. He or she then makes arrangements to submit the full text to the company concerned.

Authorlink is not a literary agency and does not retain a percentage on any deals. They charge a fee of around $120 a year for keeping your details in the Author Showcase. For authors such as June Park who recently signed a six-figure contract with HarperCollins, this is clearly a very good investment.

Author's Showcase
www.light-communications.com/author/index.html
Author's Showcase describes itself as 'an online bookstore of published and self-published authors who showcase their books with pictures, sample text, and ordering information.' For an annual fee of around $400 they will create a page for your book and, they claim, market it actively to readers, agents and publishers.

You can also put unpublished typescripts (Including work in progress) on the site for agents and publishers to peruse. Author's Showcase offers a range of additional services to help you finish and publish/self-publish your book, including copy editing, proof-reading, electronic publishing, and so on.

Author's Showcase claims 200,000 'hits' (visitors to their site) every month. They publicise authors' work by submitting details to the main search engines. They also send press releases, take out classified advertisements, and distribute information through internet mailing lists and newsgroups. See Figure 35.

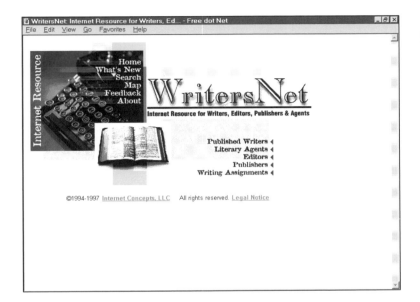

Fig. 34. Writers Net home page.

WritersNet
www.writers.net

WritersNet is a free service designed to help professional writers looking for additional assignments and commissions. To have your details included, you must have had at least one book published during the last seven years; three short stories or poems in the last five years; or three articles in the last eighteen months. You must also be prepared to check your email frequently. See Figure 34.

WritersNet has two main sections: the *Internet Directory of Published Writers*, and the *Internet Directory of Literary Agents*. The former is a searchable database of hundreds of published writers, each entry including a list of published works and biographical/contact information. The latter is a searchable directory of literary agents. Each entry

Fig. 35. The Author's Showcase home page.

contains a description of the agency, areas of specialisation, and contact information. Both writers and agents can add to or edit their entries online. A further directory, the *Internet Database of Writing Assignments*, is planned and may be available by the time you read this.

Typical examples

▷ *Lucien gets a second bite of the cherry* – An experienced author of self-help books, Lucien is frustrated by the poor sales of one of his early titles, 'How to Find the Woman of Your Dreams'. The original publisher made only a half-hearted attempt at selling this book, and gave up when initial orders were disappointing. Lucien decides to try selling an updated version via an online publisher, and is pleased when it sells steadily, if not spectacularly. Then a traditional publisher sees the book online, and offers Lucien a contract to publish the book conventionally.

▷ *Candy offers her romance on the net* – Candy is an unpublished author trying to sell her first novel, a romance set in the 1890s. She pays a fee to have a page on a site showcasing new authors' work. She gets one or two approaches from vanity publishers who praise her work in fulsome terms and offer to publish her book for a large fee. Then she receives a polite email expressing interest from a London agent. Looking her name up in the *Writers' and Artists' Yearbook*, Candy is thrilled to find out that the agent represents some of the best-known names in romantic fiction. She prints out a copy of the typescript, sends it to her office, and waits with fingers crossed.

Setting up your own writer's home page

So far, this chapter has focused on ways you can use resources which are already on the net to help market yourself and your work. But there is another, very effective, step you can take to boost your writing career, and that is set up your own home page. This is a site of your own on the web, which anyone in the world can visit as long as they have your URL.

As part of their subscription package, most ISPs will give you a megabyte or more of web space to set up your own home page. Unless you want to go mad with video, animations, sound files and such like, this should be more than adequate. What's more, modern web authoring programs make constructing web pages a relatively simple and painless process.

Subject to very few restrictions (mostly to do with avoiding anything illegal), you can use your web space as you wish. For writers, this is an opportunity that should not be missed. Here are just a few reasons why you should set up a home page of your own.

How having your own home page will help you

1. Your home page can function as an online CV

Rather than sending out multiple copies of your CV, simply provide the URL of your home page to prospective clients. This has a number of advantages: it saves time; saves the cost of postage and stationery; and shows the client you are well clued-up on new technology. It is, however, as well to check with the publisher that he has internet access first.

2. You can provide samples of your writing on the net

If publishers want to see examples of your work, you can refer them to your home page – again, saving time and money on the conventional method of sending work in the post. This can also be an opportunity to 'test market' your writing and get feedback on works in progress. Simply post a sample of your current project and ask for comments.

3. You can include quick links to your favourite web sites

Set your home page to load when you log on to the internet. You will then have a list of all your top sites with hyperlinks to take you straight to them. You can, of course, do something similar with bookmarks/favourites lists on your browser, but with your own home page you have unlimited flexibility. You can arrange the links exactly as you want them, and provide brief descriptions of each site if you wish.

4. You can form links and friendships with other writers

The internet is a vast online community. As long as you publicise your site adequately (to be discussed shortly), other writers and readers are sure to come calling. You can provide an email link to enable other people to contact you with queries, comments, ideas, proposals and so on.

5. You can market your services as a writer

Your home page can be a low cost 'billboard' advertising your services to potential clients across the world. It is open for business 24 hours a day, and effectively free of charge (in so far as you would be paying the ISP for internet access anyway).

6. You can help loyal readers keep in touch with you

Readers like to know what their favourite authors are doing. A home page lets you keep in touch without the hassle of writing to everyone personally. If you provide an email link, readers will be able to write in to you with comments and suggestions. And, of course, by encouraging reader loyalty, you should be guaranteeing yourself further sales in the future!

7. You can generate publicity and media interest

By telling local papers and writing magazines about your home page,

Examples of real author sites

you may be able to generate extra free publicity for yourself. This applies at present, though as web home pages for writers become commonplace they may become less newsworthy. It will, of course, always help if you have some novel and innovative content on your page, or if the things you write are intrinsically interesting. To give an admittedly simplistic example, a writer of erotic novels may find it easier to generate interest in her web site than a writer of business reports!

Disadvantages of having a home page

There are, admittedly, a few potential disadvantages to having a web home page. They include the following:

1. It may generate unproductive and time-consuming correspondence.

2. Creating and maintaining the site can eat into time when you would otherwise be working on paid assignments.

3. Simply having a home page is no guarantee that anyone will visit it – you will also have to spend some time and effort publicising your page.

Examples of real-life author web sites

Nevertheless, for most writers the benefits of having a home page will greatly outweigh the drawbacks. For evidence of this, you need only see how many writers, well-known and not-so-well-known, have set up sites. Just a few examples include:

Judy Blume
www.judyblume.com

Jane Dorner
www.editor.net

Ray Girvan
www.users.zetnet.co.uk/rgirvan/

Hal Gordon
home.erols.com/gordonhc/

Anne McCaffrey
arrogant.itc.icl.ie/AnneMcCaffrey.html

Michael Horovitz
www.connectotel.com/PoetryOlympics/horovitz.html

All the above are well worth visiting to see how a home page can be used to good effect. For more examples of sites by (and about) writers, see the list in Chapter 9.

How do you create a web page?

All web sites are written in a special language called HTML. This stands for hypertext mark-up language. Many good introductory books are available for people who wish to learn HTML; a number are listed in the Appendix. What follows here is a very brief introduction.

An HTML document looks like an ordinary word processing file with some additional codes written into it. The latter are designed to tell a web browser what the document is and how to display it. It is quite possible to create HTML files using an ordinary word processor. If such a file is then published on the web a browser will be able to read it, and display the page according to the formatting commands built into it.

The appearance of a web page is controlled by so-called tags. A tag is a formatting command which tells a browser how a particular feature on a web page should be displayed on screen. Tags are placed within angle brackets; they are often used in pairs. The first tag turns a feature on, and the second tag (the same, but preceded by a forward slash) turns it off again. For example, the line below would appear in bold if it were published on a web page.

<B>This sentence will appear in bold text</B>

Some other HTML text formatting codes are listed below:

<I></I>	Switches on and off italic
<U></U>	Switches on and off underline
<CENTER></CENTER>	Centres text
 	Inserts single line break
<P>	Inserts paragraph (two-line) break
<FONT SIZE=N></FONT>	Defines font size (N=1 to 7)
<HR>	Creates a screen-wide horizontal rule

Not all tags control text formatting. At the very start of the document, the <HTML> tag tells a browser that this is an HTML document, and </HTML> tells it when the end of the document has been reached. The <HEAD>, <TITLE> and <BODY> tags are used to mark out the header area, page title and main body of the page respectively. A very simple HTML document which nevertheless contains all the essential codes is shown below:

```
<HTML>
<HEAD>
<TITLE>Example document</TITLE>
</HEAD>
<BODY>
<CENTER>This is an example HTML document</CENTER>
</TITLE>
</BODY>
</HTML>
```

HTML and other web authoring tools...........................

The above is almost as simple an HTML document as it is possible to create. If saved and published on the web it would appear as a single page with the sentence 'This is an example HTML document' centred at the top of it.

Actual web pages are, of course, more complicated than this. Most include additional commands to produce images, tables, hyperlinks and so on – but the principles as described above still apply.

Examples of more complex HTML documents are easy to find. Just load any web page in your browser, and select Source (or View Source) from the View menu. You will now see in a separate window the actual HTML code your browser is using to display the page in question.

Using a web authoring package

If you wish to create your own home page, it will help if you have a basic understanding of HTML. However, the good news is that modern programs will create HTML documents for you without you having to go through the text inserting tags and so on.

If you use Microsoft Word 97, for example, you will have the option to save any document as an HTML file. Word automatically inserts the necessary tags for features such as bold and italics. You could create a simple online CV using Word 97 alone.

For a more enterprising home page – perhaps including pictures, sounds and hyperlinks – you have two choices. One is hiring someone to design the page and program it for you. There is no shortage of small businesses offering this service. If you can't find someone in your local paper or *Yellow Pages*, look at the small ads in *Internet* magazine.

The alternative is to buy an HTML writing and editing program and take the time (maybe enrolling on a course) to learn to use it. Microsoft Front Page is the market leader, but other programs such as Adobe Pagemill and HomeSite also have their adherents. Many of these popular programs are priced at around £100. It takes a while to master the many features of these programs, such as frames, but the end results should look highly professional.

If your browser is Netscape 4 (Netscape Communicator), you will also have Page Composer to create your web pages. This free package is quite powerful, and will handle text, fonts, tables, hyperlinks, backgrounds and imported images, very effectively. Netscape Communicator is on many of the CD-ROMs given away free with the popular monthly internet magazines.

Publicising your home page

As mentioned earlier, there is little virtue in having a home page if no-one ever visits it. Once your page is up and running, you should take every opportunity to publicise it. Below are a few suggestions for steps to take:

1. Advertise your web site on your letterhead and by any other means you have available.

2. Include on your site links to other sites of interest to writers. This has two benefits. First, it will make the site more useful and interesting to other writers and encourage return visits. And second, putting links on your site will help the web search engines find you.

3. Contact operators of other sites, including all those you have provided links to, asking if they will include links to your site.

4. Contact the various search engine operators to tell them about your site (but see also the item below).

5. Use the free automated submission system Submit It! to announce your new site to a range of search engines and directories. Enter

    www.submit-it.com/

    in your browser and follow the on-screen instructions.

6. Announce your site on the net-happenings mailing list run by InterNIC (the internet Network Information Centre). To announce the opening of your site, send an email to

    net-happenings@is.internic.net

7. Post a message announcing the opening of your site in appropriate newsgroups such as misc.writing. You can also include a brief plug for your site in your sig file (the 'electronic signature' at the end of any newsgroup posting or email).

8. Log on, also, to the *Internet* magazine What's New page and announce your site there:

    www.emap.com/whatsnew

It is important to make your site as interesting and informative as possible, as it is the easiest thing in the world for visitors to take one look and hyperlink somewhere else. Remember, also, to update your site at regular intervals, to encourage return visits.

How it might work . . . .

Examples

Leah's home page brings her a commission – Biographer Leah keeps a selection of her work on her home page. One day she sees a small ad in *Writers News* from an anonymous advertiser seeking a ghost writer to assist him with his autobiography. An email address is given, so Leah sends a short message expressing interest, with an invitation to the advertiser to visit her home page to find out more. The next day she gets a phone call from a well-known sportsman asking her to attend a meeting. He says that he read an extract from her work on her home page, and feels she has just the right style for his book.

Carl thinks twice about his home page – Carl, an advertising copywriter, decides to sell his services from his home page. To catch the eye of potential clients, he heads his page 'Make Big Money From Writing!' and sends details to all the search engines. When he checks his email a few days later, however, he finds it full of messages from aspiring writers and business opportunity seekers and vendors. There are no offers of any writing work. Carl decides to rethink his heading, as it is clearly attracting visitors, but not the people he wanted. He changes the heading to 'Carl Gustaffson – Advertising Copywriter'. While this is less eye-catching, he reckons it will be less apt to mislead people when the heading appears in search engine results.

6 Learning for life

In this chapter you will discover how to:

► *use online libraries and archives*
► *visit and learn from educational sites*
► *enrol on free and paid-for courses*
► *experience a 'virtual community' for writers!*

· ·

How to use online libraries and archives

Libraries have always been essential research resources for writers. However, going to your local library and poring through the shelves and card indexes can be very time-consuming – especially if the book you need is lost, out on loan, or simply not in stock. Internet users can save themselves much time and hassle by using online library and archive services.

The British Library

As a copyright library the British Library keeps copies of every book published in the UK and many published overseas. The library also has a huge collection of journals, reports, magazines, and so on. Their Portico Project (www.bl.uk) is an ambitious attempt to bring many of the British Library's resources to internet users. See Figure 36.

Various searches are available. For example OPAC 97 (Online Public Access Catalogue) is a free service which enables users to find out

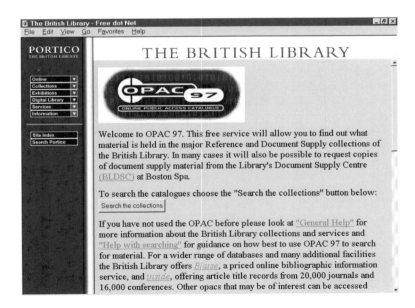

Fig. 36. British Library home page

Searching databases

what material is held in the major reference and document supply collections of the British Library. In many cases, it is also possible to request photocopies of documents from the library's Document Supply Centre at Boston Spa.

To use this service, click on the *Search the Collections* button on the OPAC 97 page (opac97.bl.uk). You will be presented with a form on which to provide search details. The information you can provide includes:

▷ author's last name

▷ author's first name or initials

▷ organisation name

▷ title phrase/keywords

▷ subject phrase/keywords

▷ publisher

▷ ISBN/ISSN

▷ date of publication

You can complete as many or as few of these search fields as you like. Click on *Begin Search*, and the site will produce a list of books and documents in the collections covered by OPAC matching your specifications. You will be able to get more information on any of these titles by clicking the number beside it.

OPAC 97 covers the major collections in the British Library. These include the humanities and social sciences collection, and the science, technology and business collection, both dating from 1975; the music collection, from 1980; and a selection of older books from the UK and overseas. It also covers the world's largest collection of conference proceedings.

For a wider range of databases and additional facilities, the British Library offers Blaise (the British Library's Automated Information Service). There is a fee for using this service, but it provides access to databases containing over 18 million bibliographic records. These range from the very first printed books to the most up-to-date scientific reports.

Blaise can be accessed in various ways. Blaise Line provides a direct line to the British Library, while Blaise Web works via the internet. Blaise covers all subject areas and all countries. Publications covered include books, reports, periodicals, conference proceedings, theses, official publications, printed sheet music and maps.

If you are compiling a bibliography or researching the published literature on any topic, Blaise can provide in seconds a comprehensive and up-to-date listing which could take weeks to research conventionally.

More information is available on the web page:

www.bl.uk/services/bsds/nbs/blaise/

National Information Services and Systems (NISS)

One problem when using the internet for research can be the difficulty of assessing the reliability of online sources. NISS (www.niss.ac.uk) aims to help net users around that problem. Through its Information Gateway, it gives access to a library of recommended web sites on any academic subject (see Figure 37).

NISS is aimed primarily at teachers, lecturers, students and research-ers. However, it can also be a useful service for writers seeking authoritative information on any area of scholarship and learning.

Each page of NISS includes a search dialog box similar to those found in search engines. To use the service, you begin by entering in this box a word or phrase identifying the subject you are interested in. Click on *Enter,* and the site generates a list of web sites which have been recommended by experts in the subject concerned. Figure 38 shows the results of a search using the term 'biology'.

If you wish, you can hyperlink straight to any site listed in the search results. However, if you want more information first, click on the *Info*

Fig. 37. The NISS home page.

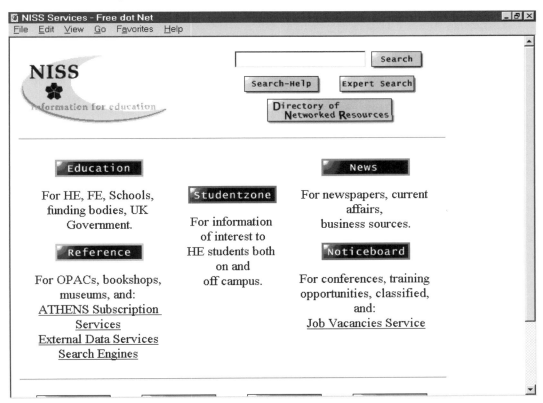

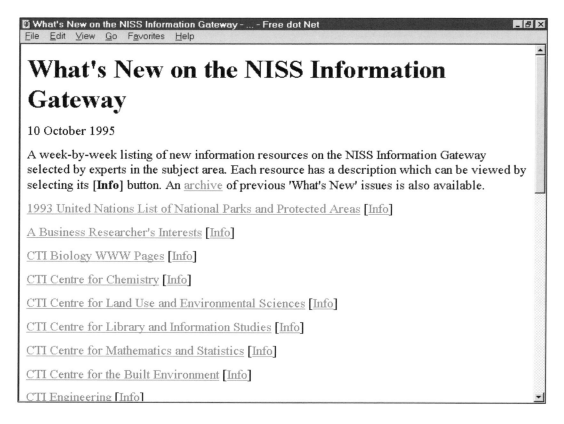

Fig. 38. A NISS results list.

link beside each title. This will show you the information from the NISS resource descriptions database concerning the site. It includes the URL, contact names, copyright details, keywords, and a description designed to help potential users decide whether the source would be of value to them. Figure 39 shows the information provided on one particular source.

Fig. 39. NISS site information.

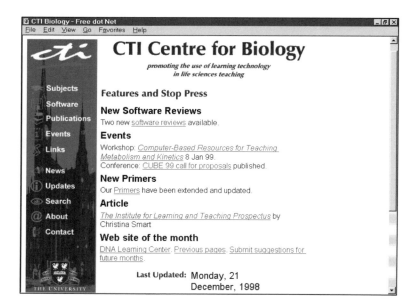

The Internet Classics Archive

The text of many out-of-copyright books is freely available on the internet. The Internet Classics Archive is at:

classics.mit.edu/titles.d.html

It includes 441 works of classical literature by 59 different writers. Most are Greek and Roman, though there are also some Chinese and Persian. All are in English translation. Greco-Roman authors with works included on the site include Aeschylus, Aesop, Antiphone, Aristotle, Julius Caesar, Cicero, Epicurus, Euclid, Galen, Herodotus, Hippocrates, Homer, Lucretius, Ovid, Plato, Plutarch, Sophocles, Virgil and Xeno-phon. Other authors listed include Confucius, Lao-tzu and Omar Khayyam.

Further information on any of the authors listed is available by clicking on the *More Info* link under each author's name. This takes you to the relevant article in the online version of *Encyclopedia Britannica*, though it should be noted that you have to pay a separate fee to use this site:

www.britannica.com

Here you can read the text of any of the works listed on-screen or save it for later study. The archive also includes search facilities, enabling

Fig. 40. The Internet Classics Archive home page.

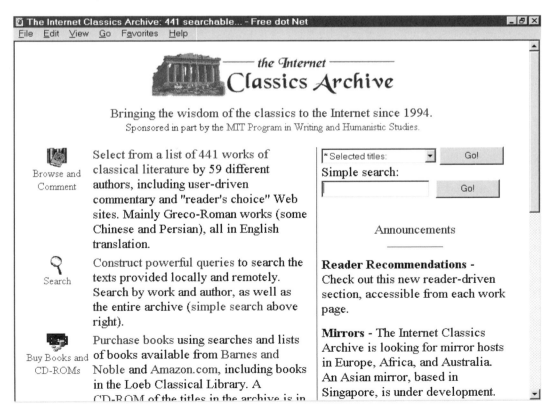

you to search for specific references in one particular title or across the whole range.

A further feature of the archive is the inclusion of reader comments on each book. You can see a list of comments, with subject headings, by clicking on the *Read Discussion* link under each title. You can click to view any of these, and a facility is provided to enable you to respond with your own comments. You are also encouraged to post a new comment to express your own views.

The Complete Works of William Shakespeare

The text of Shakespeare's plays and poetry is available at various sites on the web. This version (Figure 41) is at the site:

the-tech.mit.edu/Shakespeare/works.html

The text of all Shakespeare's plays and poems is included on this site, with search facilities similar to those in the Internet Classics Archive. An additional feature is that obscure words, or words which have changed in meaning since Shakespeare's day, are highlighted and linked to a glossary. This is a good example of how the internet can provide features unavailable in traditional publishing.

Fig. 41. The Complete Works of William Shakespeare site.

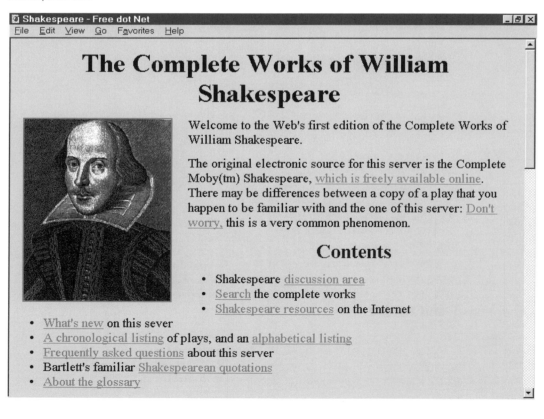

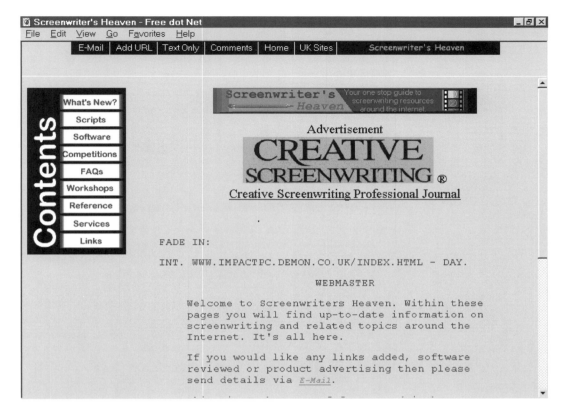

Other features on this site include a Shakespeare discussion area, a list of Shakespeare resources on the net, chronological and alphabetical listings of the plays, Bartlett's quotations from Shakespeare, and (as mentioned above) a glossary.

Fig. 42. Screenwriters Heaven home page.

Screenwriters Heaven

Screenwriters Heaven is, among other things, a script archive for screenwriters:

www.impactpc.demon.co.uk/

It is compulsory viewing for writers who dream of Hollywood. It includes links to web sites where you can find everything from treatments to finished scripts for many well-known and not-so-well-known movies. If you want to find anything from the first draft script of *Aliens* to the shooting script of *Ferris Bueller's Day Off*, this is the place to come. Other links on the site include screenwriting competitions, workshops, writers' resources and frequently asked questions.

Other library and archive sites

Libraries and archives represent a fast-growing area of internet development. This is hardly surprising when you consider the additional features web sites can offer compared with the traditional resources, such as fast searches and easy cross-referencing. Below are listed a number of other useful library and archive sites. Note that

Educational sites ....

at the time of writing some of these sites were still under development.

> *The Commonwealth War Graves Commission*
> www.cwgc.org
>
> *The Contemporary Classical Music Archive*
> www.eyeneer.com/CCM/
>
> *Drew's Script-o-Rama*
> www.script-o-rama.com
>
> *The Public Records Office*
> www.pro.gov.uk
>
> *Searchable Online Archive of Recipes*
> godzilla.eecs.berkeley.edu/recipes/
>
> The Ultimate Music Archive
> *vinnie.simplenet.com/musicarchive/*

How to visit and learn from educational sites

Whatever the subject you (or your children) want to learn, the chances are the internet has an educational site devoted to it. The best starting point is to enter a key word or phrase in one or more search engines, and see what they come up with. Here are a few interesting and informative sites to get you started.

Windows to the Universe
www.ivv.nasa.gov
Windows to the Universe is an educational web site devoted to astronomy and space exploration. From the home page, shown below, you can link to information on a wide range of topics at any of three different levels: beginner's, intermediate or advanced.

The site can be explored in various ways. For example, the left-hand frame gives access to information on the Sun and the planets of the solar system. Clicking on any of these produces a photograph of the planet concerned, a brief description and a menu leading to more detailed information. For example, the menu for Saturn has the following items:

▷ interior & surface

▷ atmosphere

▷ magnetosphere

▷ moons & rings

▷ planetary facts

▷ myth & culture

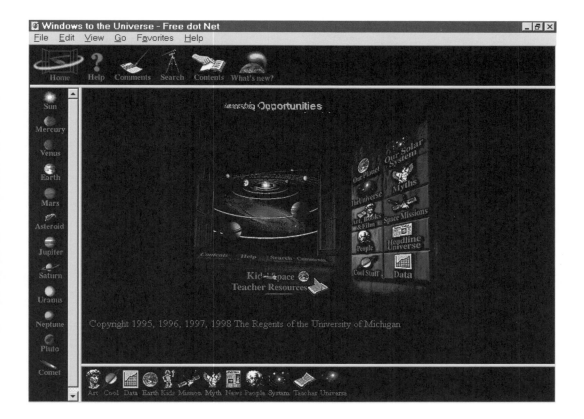

▷ space missions

▷ news & discovery

▷ image archives

Fig. 43. The Windows to the Universe home page.

Windows to the Universe is intended primarily for use by teachers and pupils. Teachers can read suggestions on the best ways to use the site, and have a facility provided to swap ideas with other teachers. Pupils can visit an area called *Cool Stuff*, which includes a range of amazing facts about astronomy.

Writers wanting to find out more about astronomy – perhaps as background for a young adults' science fiction novel – will find much here to intrigue them. The photographic images are especially striking. Though bear in mind that, with a slow modem especially, pages with photographs may take a long time to load.

Interactive Frog Dissection Kit
www-itg.lbl.gov/vfrog
The Interactive Frog Dissection Kit is one of the best-known educational sites on the web. As the name suggests, on this site you can perform a 'virtual dissection' of a frog (Figures 44 and 45). To enter the kit, click on the frog icon on the home page. The first screen you will see includes instructions on using the kit and the starting picture of 'Fluffy the Frog'. You can change the frog's size by clicking on

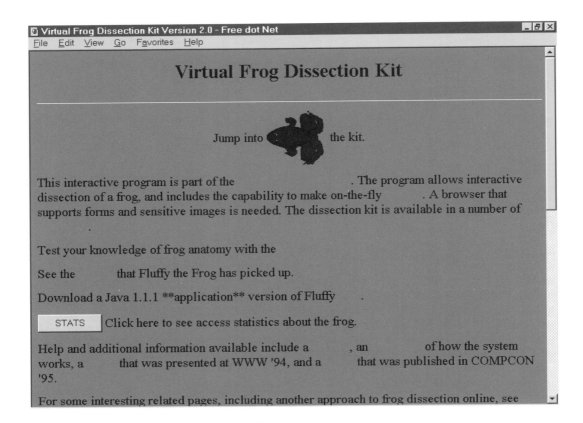

Fig. 44. Interactive Frog Dissection Kit home page.

the '+' and '-' boxes on the upper left of the image. By clicking on the icon bar at the top of the screen, you can turn the frog over or rotate it in the direction shown. Clicking on the projector icon will show the rotation as a short film (note: not all browsers will support this facility).

Fig. 45. Interactive Frog Dissection Kit – The Frog.

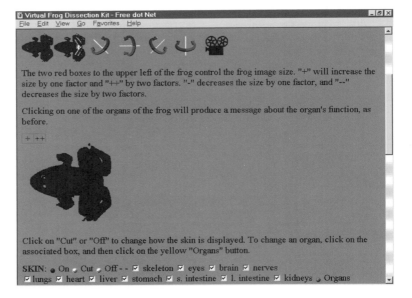

To begin the dissection, click on *SKIN - Cut* or *Off* to show the skin cut back or removed completely. Clicking over any organ will reveal its name and a short message about the organ's function. Under the frog is a list of organs, each with a check box beside it. You can remove any organ by clicking on the associated box, and then clicking the Organs button at the end of the list. By this means you can take out, and just as easily put back again, the frog's skeleton, eyes, brain, nerves, lungs, heart, liver, stomach, small and large intestines and kidneys.

Though clearly something of a novelty, The Interactive Frog Dissection Kit is a useful and cleverly programmed site. It demonstrates well the potential of the net as an educational tool.

How Do They Do That With HTML?

www.nashville.net/~carl/htmlguide/index.html
As you would expect, there are many web sites on the subject of HTML, the main programming language of the web. This one is packed with information and advice for people who want to create better-looking web pages. Although the strapline says *Answers for the novice or expert*, it is not a site for complete beginners.

The site is divided into two main sections. The first part is entitled Basic HTML and graphics. The subjects covered here are:

Fig. 46. How Do They Do That With HTML? home page

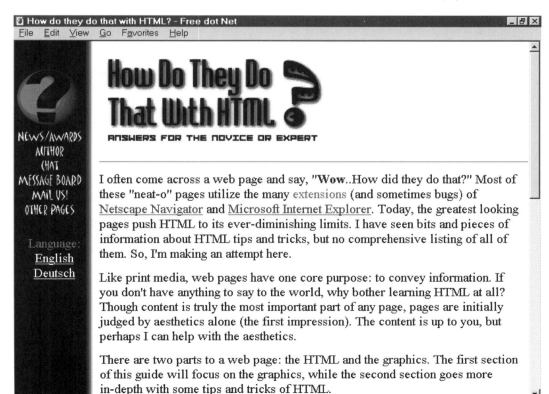

More adventurous HTML ....

  ▷ backgrounds and colours

  ▷ transparent and interlaced GIFs

  ▷ make the most of fonts

  ▷ GIF animation

  ▷ awesome graphics!

The second section is HTML tips and tricks. The subjects covered here are:

  ▷ access counters

  ▷ ... and other statistics

  ▷ quick columns

  ▷ back button

  ▷ dynamic menus

  ▷ dynamic documents

  ▷ easy browser detection

  ▷ background sounds

  ▷ HTTP cookies

  ▷ tables and frames

The advice given is concise and readable, and hyperlinks are included to other relevant sites. For example, the section on background files and colours includes links to HTML colour charts and sources of free background images. How Do They Do That With HTML? is a good information source for anyone who has written their first web page and is keen to start adding some bells and whistles.

Your questions answered

When I am studying, is it OK to copy text from web pages into my notes?

It is quite in order to copy and paste material into a word processor document for later study. If, however, you want to use the material in a published work, you will of course need to obtain permission from the copyright-holder. (See also the advice on copyright in Chapter Eight.)

Is it possible to copy images from a web site, as well as the text?

Certainly! Just right-click over the image, and select *Copy* to paste it onto the Clipboard, or *Save Image As* to save the image into the directory or folder of your choice.

Are there any good guides on the web to educational sites?

A number of web sites list and categorise educational sites, and in many cases provide original content of their own. Some key UK sites include:

Educate Online
www.educate.co.uk

Eduweb
www.eduweb.co.uk

BT Home Campus
www.campus.bt.com

BECTA
www.becta.org.uk
The British Educational Communications and Technology Agency

How about educational newsgroups and mailing lists?

Again, there are plenty of these as well. Enter your subject interest in the dialog box in Dejanews (www.dejanews.com) and you are sure to find at least one relevant newsgroup, be it alt.maths.algebra or rec.films. You can also subscribe to a mailing list such as that provided by Pacific Bell, part of the education technology department at San Diego State University (www.kn.pacbell.com/wired/blue.webn).

How to enrol on free and paid-for courses

As well as visiting educational sites, you can enrol on a range of courses on the internet. This is a fast-growing area, as colleges and universities gear up to deliver online courses to people who are un-willing or unable to attend traditional classes. Such courses may appeal to people for reasons such as the following:

(a) They do not live near a convenient study centre.

(b) They have to fit study around work or family commitments.

(c) They suffer from physical or mental disabilities which make going out difficult.

(d) They simply prefer this method of learning.

Some universities, such as Wolverhampton, are exploring the possibility of making some of their regular lectures and course material available over the internet. The potential benefits of this include

▷ savings on cost and time spent travelling to and from lectures

▷ savings of staff time delivering lectures (though extra time may have to be allocated to student support)

▷ reduced printing and photocopying expenditure

The courses currently available via the internet include some which are free and others you pay a fee for. Of course, it takes a lot of time and money to develop and programme an online course, so free courses tend to be short, experimental, or provided as free tasters for other fee-paying courses at the institution. Nevertheless, there are some worthwhile and interesting courses you can study in this way, and enrolment is generally quite straightforward.

Paid-for courses tend to be more substantial. Such courses often come as a package, combining at least some of the ingredients below.

▷ One or more web sites containing instructional material, links to other useful sites and details of assignments.

▷ a mailing list or electronic notice board

▷ a chat facility enabling students to communicate with one another over the net in real time

▷ a tutor (or team of tutors) available via email to give feedback and support

▷ face-to-face meetings and seminars

▷ the opportunity to meet and collaborate with other students

▷ printed support material

▷ special software as required

Fees for such courses vary widely, but they usually compare favourably with the cost of equivalent traditional courses. If possible, however, it is wise to contact former students to check their impressions of the course before deciding whether to part with your money.

This section of the book will examine a resource which includes links to a number of free courses (OLLiE), and a specific paid-for course (LeTTOL). Information on other online courses can be obtained in the usual way through queries to search engines and directories, posting information requests in relevant newsgroups, and visiting educational web sites.

The Online Learning Experience (OLLiE)

www.canterbury.ac.uk/cware/OLLiE/
The Online Learning Experience is a project run from the University of Kent at Canterbury. It aims to show the wide range of courseware (online learning resources) being developed within higher education. The site reveals how universities are using the net for purposes including:

▷ displaying course timetables and outlines

▷ handling student enquiries and enrolment

▷ presenting lectures and self-study material

▷ conducting student assessment

▷ supporting learners via email, newsgroups and so on.

▷ evaluating courses through student feedback

▷ making lecture notes available online

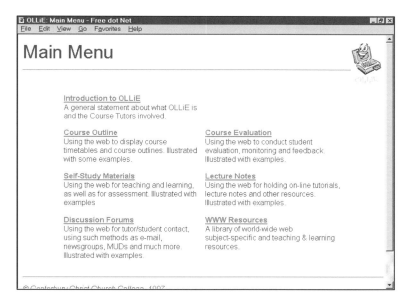

Fig. 47. The OLLiE home page.

To see a range of free online courses, click on *Self-study materials* from the home page (above). One resource linked from here is a short course entitled Break of Day in the Trenches produced by the Centre for Humanities Computing at the University of Oxford (info.ox.ac.uk/ hyppoem.html). This focuses on the well-known Great War poem by Wilfred Owen. To the poem itself is attached a wide variety of information relevant to the study of the War Poets.

Other courses you can access from OLLiE include the following:

▷ the structure of proteins
▷ food hygiene
▷ IT applications
▷ light diffraction
▷ glycolysis
▷ applied statistics for sociologists
▷ history of mathematics
▷ medical tutorial on the knee
▷ online statistics course for sociology
▷ the UMDS teaching radiology file

▷ obstetric ultrasound teaching file

▷ operating systems course

Some of these are free-standing courses for internet-users, but others are really for use by students on conventional, fee-paying courses. Nevertheless, you can still visit the sites and access the study materials free of charge.

Learning to Teach Online (LeTTOL)

www.sheffcol.ac.uk/lettol/index.htm

Learning to Teach Online is a paid-for course developed by South Yorkshire Networks for Enterprise, a collaboration between the eight further education colleges in South Yorkshire. The fee at the time of writing is £275.

The course is intended for teachers, lecturers, trainers and academic managers. It is intended to provide an opportunity for course members to gain an understanding of how online learning works, and equips participants to:

▷ teach and support learners online

▷ manage online learning provision

Fig. 48. The LeTTOL home page.

▷ apply suitable learning methods in the design of online learning materials

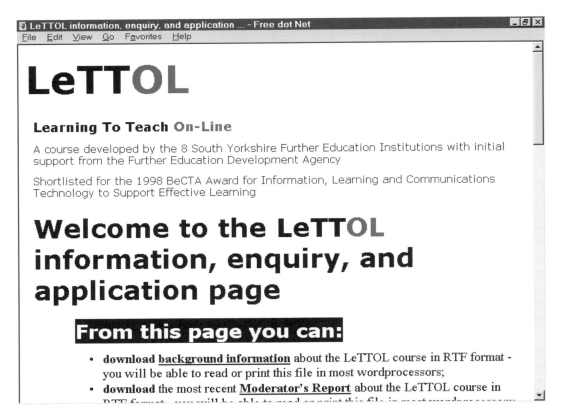

The majority of LeTTOL course activities, tutor support, interaction with other students and assessment take place online. LeTTOL involves approximately 90 guided learning hours, spread over a period of about four months. Open College Network credits are provided to students who complete the course successfully. The outline for the course is as follows:

> Unit 1 – *Getting started*
> Working online
> How the course will work
> Getting to know each other
>
> Unit 2 – *Learning online*
> Distance learning
> From theory into practice
> Online resources
>
> Unit 3 – *Learning management issues*
> Learner support
> Assessment
>
> Unit 4 – *Online design and delivery*
> Designing online activities
> Designing online courses

The course involves a series of activities or assignments. Early ones involve straightforward tasks such as writing a short piece about yourself and sending it to your tutor as an email attachment, while later assignments involve designing online learning activities, and developing course outlines.

A feature of the course is the way students are encouraged to interact with one another via email and First Class, a kind of electronic bulletin board. Course members are allocated to small groups and exchange and comment on one another's work, as well as contributing towards group projects.

LeTTOL is a good example of a paid-for course which operates mainly online (some resources are provided in printed form, and there are optional face-to-face meetings). Students from Canada, Australia, South Africa, Singapore and Italy have enrolled on the course, showing that, when studying via the internet, geographical distance need be no barrier.

Clearly, a course such as LeTTOL will be of interest only to a minority of writers (though many writers do also teach, and increasingly may wish to pass on their skills and knowledge via the internet). Nevertheless, the course has been described in some detail here to give readers a flavour of what studying an online course entails.

Joining a virtual community or forum.............................

The pros and cons of online courses

Pros
1. can study from your own home at times convenient to yourself

2. able to use online facilities such as email and the world wide web

3. good potential for collaborative learning

4. cost savings in terms of travel

Cons
1. paying for internet access and phone calls pushes up the cost

2. may be problems of compatibility and lack of technical support

3. lack of personal contact with tutors and fellow students may cause feelings of isolation

4. easy to fall behind with studies if you are not well organised and self-disciplined

How to join a virtual community for writers

A virtual community is a place on the internet where people with something in common (such as a shared interest in writing) can meet and interact in various ways. You *could* say a mailing list or newsgroup was a community, but the term is usually reserved for sites which offer a range of information and services for the people concerned.

To confuse the issue further, not all such sites call themselves communities. Another term used by some internet access providers is forums. An example is the Writers Forum hosted by CompuServe (www.compuserve.com). See Figure 49. This is accessible only to people who use CompuServe for internet access, but other providers

Fig. 49. CompuServe
Writers Forum home page

such as AOL (www.aol.com) and CIX (www.cix.co.uk) offer similar services for their subscribers.

The CompuServe Writers Forum offers a range of resources and facilities for writers. To begin with, there is the file library. This is a collection of files you can read or download to your computer. Files can include articles, interviews, software, graphics, and so on. At the time of writing, files were on offer in the following categories:

general information	writers tools	writers hotline
markets	self-publishing	contest: whodunnit?
writer-of-the-month	students and teachers	writers registry
workshop – novels	essays and opinions	conferences and shows
workshop – short stories	art of writing	technical writing
writing exercises	stage/theatre	internet resources
non-English	film and television	
research and craft	the critical view	

List of categories in the CompuServe Writers Forum File Library

Message boards are another facility on offer at the CompuServe Writers Forum. These operate rather like newsgroups. Messages can be posted under headings similar to those in the file libraries list (above). You can read the messages and reply to any of them, and you can also post a message of your own. Some themes and topics featuring on message boards at the time of writing included:

▷ a discussion on the merits of writing for pleasure vs writing for money

▷ a request from an overworked technical writer for someone to assist him with writing reviews and articles

▷ a query about the correct format for film and TV scripts

▷ some (constructive) critical feedback about a chapter of a novel posted on the forum

▷ an appeal from an electronic publishing company for book-length submissions

▷ several requests from authors for publishers

▷ an invitation from a playwright to fellow members to come to a rehearsed reading of her latest play

▷ an enquiry about internet writers' clubs

Geocities and virtual neighbourhoods ....

The CompuServe Writers Forum also hosts regular conferences. These are live interactions with other members. They are similar to phone calls, except you type instead of talk. Forum conferences enable you to meet and converse with other Forum members.

Some conferences feature a guest speaker in a question-and-answer format. These conferences are moderated, which means there is someone (the moderator) who acts as chair and decides whose question will be taken next. Some big name authors such as Dean Koontz and Stephen King have taken part in such conferences, and the transcripts are later posted in the forum file libraries.

As well as the Writers Forum, CompuServe members interested in writing can join other relevant forums such as the Authors Forum and Fleet Street Forum (an area for professional journalists). Forum membership is free of charge, though you do, of course, have to pay the subscription fee to the internet access provider concerned.

Geocities

www.geocities.com
Geocities represents a rather different approach to communities. This US-based company offers free personal home pages on the web, and help in creating them, to anyone in the world with web access. It does not provide access itself, so to use the facilities you would need to subscribe via another internet access provider.

The company also offers free email accounts for its residents. It claims to have more than 2.4 million individuals signed up, creating one of the largest – and most diverse – clusters of sites on the web. Your free home page can be set up in any of GeoCities' 41 themed communities. Those which may be of most interest to writers include:

Area 51 – science fiction and fantasy
Athens – education, literature, poetry, philosophy
Broadway – theatre, musicals, show business
College Park – university life
Eureka – small businesses, home offices
Hollywood – film and TV
Madison Avenue – advertising
Paris – romance, poetry, the arts
SoHo – art, poetry, prose, the bohemian spirit
Television City – TV fan clubs, sitcoms, talk shows

Many writers choose to set up home in the Athens community. The welcome page describes this area in the following terms: Athens is a community of philosophers, teachers, and other thinkers, with a wide range of spiritual and ethical beliefs. Athens is an open forum, united by a tolerant attitude and the right to free speech. The Atrium serves as a gathering place for equal citizens in this neighborhood named for the

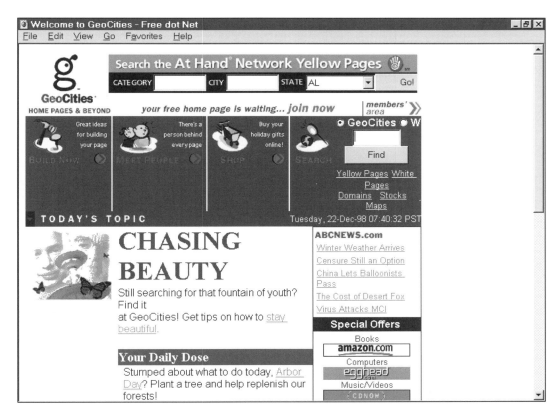

Fig. 50. The Geocities home page.

bed of democracy. No one judging another, but acknowledging those who wish to make their voice heard within the community.

The community is further divided into avenues, for writers, artists, philosophers, and so on. The residents of each avenue are indexed alphabetically, with brief information about what their page contains and a hyperlink to take you there. A selection from the writers index, illustrating the wide range of purposes people use their home pages for, is shown below:

▷ Allsorts – an online novel about life, living and becoming by Gerry Coughlan.

▷ AthenaPrime – described as a journey through the heart and spirit, this is a site for finding information about romance and witchcraft.

▷ Raina Lynn's home page – tips for budding novelists and information on Raina's own novels.

▷ The Character Refugee Center – an ongoing fantasy novel written by four people through email, including glossaries of characters, countries, objects, and authors.

▷ Haven – a science fiction and fantasy email writing club. Members write stories set in Haven, a city of cut-throats, thieves, assassins, merchants, soldiers, and other unusual characters.

▷ Some Collected Writings by Mikael Colville-Andersen – a collection of travel writing and short fiction in English by the Danish writer Mikael Colville-Andersen.

Examples ....

▷ Soothsayer Hollow – writers and writing, featured short story writers, book reviews, links to literary magazines, and other resources for writers.

Some people may feel that GeoCities stretches the community metaphor further than they are wholly comfortable with. Even if you are not convinced of the merits of becoming a virtual resident in a virtual community, however, GeoCities can provide an easy way of setting up your writing home page (especially if your ISP does not provide free web space). It is also a good place to find people with similar interests, or simply to browse and explore.

Typical examples

1. *William gets his book on the right track* – William, a retired train driver, wants to turn his years of experience on the railways into a novel. He joins the CompuServe Writers Forum, and reads all the articles on novel writing in the file library. As his novel takes shape, he finds he has problems with matters such as dialogue and characterisation. He posts queries on the message boards, and receives encouraging replies from more experienced writers. When he is sufficiently confident he posts a chapter from the novel on a message board and invites comments. He gets a range of responses, including an enthusiastic message from a literary agent asking to see the entire book.

2. *Shashi escapes from her garret* – Shashi, a budding poet, has no-one she can discuss her art with. She decides to set up a home page in GeoCities' Paris community. Though she has no prior experience of programming, with the aid of the free tools available from GeoCities she has soon created a simple but attractive site. She includes a number of her poems, with notes on how they were written and information about herself. Within a few weeks she receives emails from several fellow GeoCities residents complimenting her on her work and offering constructive criticism. Some send samples of their own poetry, and Shashi enjoys reading and commenting on them. Within a short time she is hosting an email poetry writers' circle with plans for an anthology and other joint projects.

7 Getting more benefit

In this chapter you will discover how to:

▶ *get useful software from the internet*
▶ *make use of internet faxing and telephony*
▶ *translate your work and other people's*
▶ *use online bookshops*

. . . .

How to get useful software from the internet

It's not just information you can get from the net. All kinds of useful software (computer programs) are available as well. The process for obtaining this involves logging on to an internet site and having the program sent to you electronically via your phone line and modem – a process known as downloading.

Software is normally downloaded from the net by means of a process called **file transfer protocol** (ftp). Modern browsers can handle ftp seamlessly. Often the only sign that you are logging on to an ftp site will be that the URL in the status bar at the bottom of the browser screen begins with the letters ftp rather than http.

What software can you get?

Some software available on the net you have to pay for, though much is available free. To obtain software for which a fee is payable, you will normally have to enter your credit/debit card details on an online order form. Some people are uneasy about this; but modern data encryption technology means it is highly unlikely your card number will fall into the wrong hands.

Free software falls into two main categories

▷ shareware

▷ freeware

Shareware

Shareware is software you can use free of charge for a limited period (usually a month or so). After this time, if you have found find the program useful, you are asked to register and send a fee to the publisher. This will entitle you to continue using the program, and may bring other benefits such as upgrades and a printed user manual.

Some shareware programs automatically cut out after a set period such as thirty days. Others have certain features missing or incapacitated, and you have to register to obtain the full version. In some cases a reminder screen pops up at intervals asking you to register; should you choose to ignore this, however, you may still be able to go on using the program.

Shareware is really a way of obtaining software 'on approval' to see whether it would be of use to you. As such, it is a system that benefits both producers and consumers. If you obtain a shareware program and like it, it is well worth paying the modest fee (typically £20–£30) to register. Not only will this entitle you to the latest version of the program, by playing fair you help to ensure that the shareware system continues to everyone's mutual benefit.

Freeware

As the name suggests, freeware is software which can be downloaded and used free of charge. Why would any company choose to give programs away? There are three main reasons:

1. One is that they also sell a paid-for version with extra features. The company hopes that if you like the freeware, you will be prepared to splash out for the full commercial version.

2. Another possible reason is that the program is still being developed; the company gives it away as a market research exercise in the hope of getting feedback from users.

3. And finally, there are some individuals who simply enjoy developing software, and are willing to give their programs away to anyone who can make use of them. An example of this is so-called 'postcardware', in which satisfied users are asked to send the developer a thank-you card!

Downloading WinZip

WinZip is a well known and widely used shareware file-compression and decompression tool. It is used here as an example of the typical process involved in downloading software from the internet. It is quite simple to use.

Why would you want to download WinZip? Well, with it you can 'compress' files so that they take up much less space on your computer. This can be useful if space on your hard disk is limited; but it is mainly relevant when dealing with files from the internet.

Because large files can take an age to transmit across the net, many of them are provided in 'zipped' (compressed) format. You need a program such as WinZip to unzip such files after you have downloaded them so that you can make use of them.

WinZip is also useful if you have to send a large file – such as the text of your novel – via the internet. If you zip it first, it will take much less time to send and less time to download at the other end. The recipient will, of course, need WinZip or a similar program in order to unzip your file and read it.

To download WinZip, your first need to access the web site:

www.winzip.com

Enter this URL into your browser, and you should see the WinZip home page (Figure 51).

To download the shareware program, click on *Download Evaluation Version*. This will take you to the download page. Click on *Download WinZip*, and WinZip will automatically be downloaded to your computer.

A dialog box will appear once the entire file has been transferred asking in which folder/directory you want to save WinZip. You can accept the program's suggestion (which is generally perfectly sensible), or enter an alternative of your own. Once you have done this, the program will automatically be installed on to your computer. If you wish, you can start using it immediately.

Other programs available from the internet

Many programs can be obtained over the net. The following is a

Fig. 51. WinZip home page.

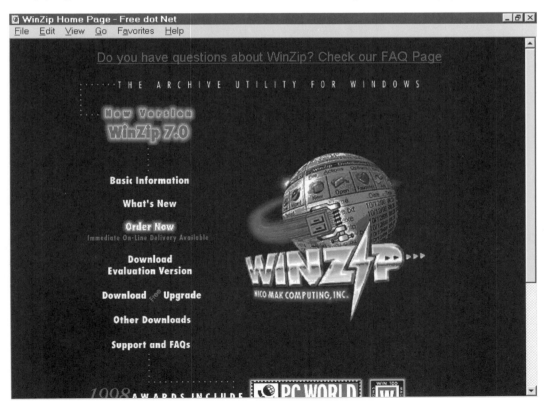

Useful programs from the internet ....

selection. Some are shareware, some freeware, and some you have to pay for.

Arachnophilia
www.arachnoid.com/lutusp/arach.html
This is a useful, free tool for building web pages. It takes formatted text, tables and outlines from any Windows 95 application and converts them to HTML.

BookMarx
www.msw.com.au
This free program monitors your bookmarks or favourites, and lets you know when a link changes or dies.

Cooledit 96
www.syntrillium.com
This is an inexpensive audio editing program which can be used for a wide range of purposes, from producing a sound file for your web page to editing the soundtrack of your promotional video.

Handy Email 1.0
www.primasoft.com
This is a simple and efficient free email program which works with Windows 95, 98 and NT.

InfoFerret
www.ferretsoft.com/netferret/products.htm
This freeware program allows you to interrogate a number of search engines quickly and conveniently. A paid-for version, more powerful and with a wider range of facilities, can also be downloaded from the web site.

Murl
murl.com
Murl is a free program which lets you store your internet bookmarks on the web, so you can find your favourite sites easily whatever computer you happen to be using.

Opera
www.operasoftware.com
This is an unusual item, a browser you have to pay for. It is faster and lighter than Netscape Navigator and Microsoft internet Explorer, and has a range of useful features.

Paint Shop Pro
www.jasc.com
This is one of the best graphics programs available, especially if you want to create attractive-looking web pages. It is available in various versions, with moderate fees payable in every case.

Real Audio Player
www.real.com
This popular free plug-in allows you to receive audio and video broadcasts via your web browser.

ReGet Pro
www.reget.com
This program is designed for people who regularly download large files and want to avoid the annoyance of having to start again when a download is cut off. ReGet Pro is designed to integrate with Internet Explorer 4. The price is $20 (around £12.50).

SmartDraw
www.smartdraw.com
This is a business drawing package, which can be used to create flow charts, tables of organisation, floor plans, presentations and so on. The current price is £34.95.

Software sources on the net

You can obtain a wide range of software from certain web sites. Programs are available for Macintosh computers as well as IBM-compatible PCs. Software for the latter includes programs which work with all versions of the Microsoft Windows operating system (3.x, 95, 98, and NT). The following sources are all well worth trying.

Download.com
www.download.com
A massive library of shareware and freeware.

Dr Download
www.drdownload.com
This site contains a smaller selection of what it reckons are the best shareware programs currently available.

Freeware Now
www.freewarenow.com
As the name says, a top source for freeware.

Jumbo
www.jumbo,com
All kinds of programs can be found here, divided into a number of major categories.

Hot Files
www.hotfiles.com
This is another internet shareware library. All their programs are checked and guaranteed virus-free.

Rat Loaf
www.ratloaf.com
If you want a new screensaver, this is the place to come.

Writers' software

Thompson Partnership
www.ttp.co.uk
This is the home page of the Thompson Partnership, a major distributor of UK shareware.

Writers' software on the net

As well as the general purpose programs mentioned earlier, you can also obtain software specifically for writers via the internet. The following is a selection of what is available. Note that in some cases you cannot download the program directly from the net, but have to send for it. The web page in these cases may contain an online order form, or simply information and details of how to order by conventional mail.

ComedyWriter for Windows
members.aol.com/index/comedy.htm
This is a brainstorming tool designed to help writers come up with humorous scenes, dialogue, characters, and so on. It includes a large database of first names. A fee is payable, but a free demonstration version can be downloaded from the web site.

Hollywood Screenplay
www.writerspage.com/hsbase.htm
This is a word processing program which automatically performs the task of formatting and paginating screenplays, TV sitcoms, and stage plays, US style. Fee payable.

Paper Chase
(www.valon.demon.co.uk/pc/pchase.htm
This is a general purpose program for writers by *Writers News* columnist Kye Valongo. It includes market information with free updates, standard query letters, manuscript tracking, and so on. A fee is payable.

SAMM
www.utahlinx.com/users/kcummings/SAMM.htm
This is an author's manuscript management program, written by Kevin Cummings and available as freeware.

StoryCraft
www.writerspage.com/software.htm
StoryCraft is a story development tool for novelists and screenplay writers. The software is based on the Jarvis Method, a mythological approach to writing fiction. A fee is payable, but there is a free demo/brochure on the web site.

The Working Writer
www.wp.com/writers.html
This is a query, submission, market and agent tracking system for writers. A fee is payable, but a free demonstration version can be downloaded from the web site.

The Writer's Software Companion
www.novalearn.com
This tutorial by Nancy Kress, a columnist with the well-respected US magazine *Writer's Digest*, uses 'total immersion technology' to accelerate a writer's progress. A fee is payable.

Other sources

In addition to the above, if you subscribe through an internet service provider such as Compuserve or AOL, it is well worth checking out the software available in their writers' forums or communities.

The web sites listed under 'Software sources on the net' should also be checked to see what programs for writers they have available. In particular, shareware and freeware dictionaries, thesauri, word processors and so on should be readily available from these sources.

Finally, here is an American site well worth trying for writers' software:

Starcomp
www.leonardo.net/starcomp/index.html
They sell a wide range of programs for writers, including plot and character assistants, script formatters, aids to budgeting and scheduling, and so on. Many are available for less than the usual commercial price.

Virus precautions

Computer viruses, unfortunately, are a fact of life. Once they have found their way on to your computer, their effects can range from nothing at all to wiping your hard disk.

The usual mode of transmission for viruses is through executable programs. These are ones whose file-names generally end '.exe'. Most data and word processing files cannot carry viruses; though there is an important exception, in that Microsoft Word files may carry so-called macro viruses.

When you run an infected program, the virus is activated and wreaks whatever havoc it can. Before running any program, therefore – whether from a shop, the internet or the cover disk of a computer magazine – you should *always* use a virus checker before running it.

Viruses are discussed in more detail in Chapter 8.

How to make use of internet faxing and telephony

Faxing (or facsimile transmission, to give it its proper name) and telephony are of course older technologies than the internet. Nevertheless, the net can help make both cheaper and more convenient, especially over long distances.

Internet faxing . . . .

Sending and receiving faxes

Traditionally, if you wanted to send and receive faxes you had to have a fax machine and a second, dedicated phone line. You could, of course, get a combination fax/answering machine, but even the best of these have their limitations. For the typical writer working from home, the internet may have the ideal solution.

Oddly enough, for writers with their own computers, sending faxes is not usually a problem. Most modern word processors have the facility to 'print' word processing documents as fax messages. In addition, modems are invariably supplied with software enabling you to fax directly from your computer. A greater problem can be having a method for conveniently receiving faxes, especially when they arrive unexpectedly.

The leading supplier of internet fax services is JFAX (www.jfax.com). Unlike some other services, the JFAX service enables you to receive faxes at any time, not just send them (Figure 52).

Fig. 52. The JFAX home page.

When you open an account with JFAX, you are given a number to quote for people wishing to send you faxes. This number may be in London (which will probably be top choice for UK writers), or around 100 other cities across the world. These include New York, Berlin,

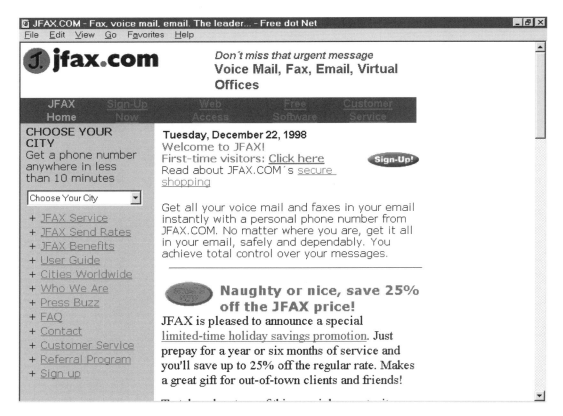

Chicago, Dublin, Paris, Brussels, Amsterdam, Sydney, Frankfurt, Toronto, and so on.

When someone sends you a fax, it is automatically converted into the JFAX format and sent to your normal email address. When you open your email, the fax is automatically decoded using software provided by JFAX. You can then read the fax on screen and, if you wish, print it out. You can also send faxes using JFAX – though as there is an extra charge for this, it is only likely to be relevant if you need to send a fax to another country.

One other aspect of the JFAX service is that as well as faxes, callers can also leave voicemail messages on your designated number. These are similarly converted to JFAX format, and sent to you via email. When you download your email, any voicemail files can be played back like answerphone messages.

At the time of writing, the JFAX service costs $12.50 (around £7.50) a month. There is also a one-off joining fee of $15 (around £9). For this you can receive unlimited faxes and voicemails. Members of some internet service providers such as CompuServe and AOL can get one month's trial of the JFAX service free of charge.

Pros and cons of JFAX internet faxing

Pros
▷ inexpensive alternative to dedicated fax machine/phone line
▷ can have fax/voicemail numbers in London, USA, Paris, etc.
▷ no noise or disruption if faxes arrive in the middle of the night
▷ faxes arrive on computer – no need to print out unless you wish
▷ unwanted 'junk faxes' are easily deleted
▷ savings on international call charges when sending faxes overseas

Cons
▷ only London numbers are currently available in the UK
▷ monthly fee may be expensive if you send and receive few faxes
▷ need to log on to the internet to send and receive faxes
▷ you won't know till you log on whether or not you have received a fax

Your questions answered

Are there any other fax services on the internet?

There are alternatives to JFAX for sending faxes (see below), but not so many for receiving them. However, some ISPs are starting to offer this in their range of services for subscribers. One such is Demon internet (www.demon.net). They have a system similar to JFAX called Dfax.

Making phone calls over the internet ....

With Dfax incoming faxes are converted to gif files, then sent as email attachments. At the time of writing the fee for Demon subscribers is £10 a month, and there is an additional one-off charge of £19.99 plus VAT for the Dfax service.

Can I send faxes free via the net?

Yes, you can. Try TPC Fax, available from:

www.tpc.int

This service lets you send 'free' faxes to most parts of the world via email – your only cost is the local call for the internet connection. If you download the free HQFax program, you can fax direct from your word processor. TPC Fax can actually be a cost-effective way of sending faxes in the UK as well. The only catch is that the cover sheet of your fax will have an advertisement included on it.

So should I scrap my old fax machine now?

The answer depends on whether you have a scanner. If not, you will have problems faxing printed magazine articles, photos and so on. With a scanner you can save these items electronically. Then anything you can do with a fax machine, you can do at least as easily (and often more cheaply) over the net.

Internet telephony

The internet makes it possible to send faxes across the world for the cost of a local call. It should therefore come as no surprise that it is possible to make low cost international phone calls as well. Various companies provide this service, but a good starting point is Delta Three (see Figure 53).

Delta Three
www.deltathree.com
Delta Three is a US-based internet telephony company. Using their PC-to-phone service, you can make calls from your computer to over 200 countries across the world. The way this works is as follows:

1. You make your call using the special dialling software.

2. Your speech is converted to digital form by your computer.

3. The signal is then compressed and transported over the internet.

4. The signal reaches the Delta Three telephone gateway in your destination country.

5. The gateway changes the signal so that it will be recognised by an ordinary phone, and forwards it via the local phone lines.

6. The recipient receives your call and hears your voice exactly as though the call had been made conventionally.

The price you pay will comprise your usual local fee for internet access plus Delta Three's own call charges. The latter, however, are low by UK standards. For example, you can phone anywhere in the US or Canada for 10 cents a minute (about 6p). Add this to the typical UK off-peak local charge of 1p a minute, and you have a total cost of 7p a minute for phoning anywhere in North America.

Some other Delta Three charges in cents and (approximate) sterling equivalents are listed below. All prices are per minute and apply at any time of the day or night.

	US Dollars	Pounds
Australia	0.14	0.08
France	0.14	0.08
Germany	0.13	0.08
India	0.86	0.52
Jamaica	0.63	0.38
Kenya	0.85	0.51
Norway	0.10	0.06
United Kingdom	0.12	0.07

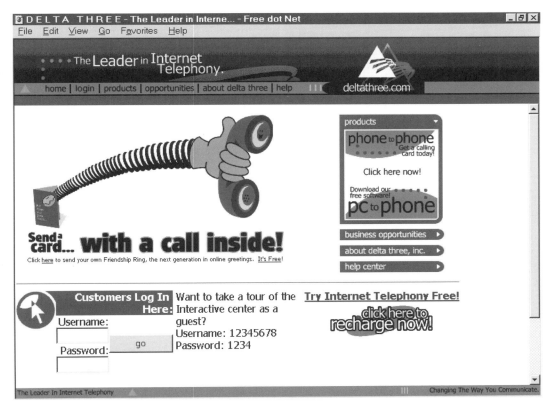

Fig. 53. The Delta Three home page.

Delta Three . . . .

To use the Delta Three service, you will need a reasonably modern computer (Pentium 75 MHz or higher) running Windows 95/98 or NT. You will also need a microphone and speakers, or a microphone headset. In addition, you will require the free dialler software available for downloading from the Delta Three web site.

Once you have registered for a Delta Three account and installed the free software, you can make phone calls from your PC to almost any regular phone (not mobiles) in the world.

Pros and cons of internet phones

Pros

▷ generally cheaper than standard phones
▷ same rates at all times of day
▷ no hassle with long-distance calls
▷ dialling codes and other useful information provided online
▷ with US companies no VAT or other taxes to pay

Cons

▷ sound quality is not always as good as standard phones
▷ may not be any cheaper for calling some countries
▷ need to make payments over the internet by credit card
▷ need to add cost of local call for internet access to internet telephony charges

Your questions answered

I use a Macintosh rather than an IBM-compatible PC. Can I use the Delta Three telephony service?

Yes, but you will need to obtain different dialling software, as Delta Three's only works with PCs. You can obtain suitable software from a company called Vocaltec:

www.vocaltec.com

Their internet Phone version 3.5 for use with Macs will work with Delta Three's PC-to-phone service.

How do I pay for calls?

With Delta Three you make pre-payments from your credit card. You can choose to make $25, $50 or $100 pre-payments. All rates are quoted in US dollars, but your credit card will be charged the equivalent in pounds sterling or whatever currency is used in your country. This becomes your balance, and the cost of each call is then deducted from that balance.

How does Delta Three calculate the cost of each call?

They bill in six-second increments according to the rates mentioned above. For example, if one call's duration is 10 minutes and 6 seconds, you will be charged for 10 minutes +0.1 of a minute. If the call was 10 minutes and 5 seconds, you will be billed for just 10 minutes.

How to translate your work and other people's

Whether you want to translate your own work into another language, or another language into English, the internet is sure to be able to help you – with an initial rough translation, at least. For a straightforward translation of words from one language to another, try Research-It!

Research-It!
www.itools.com/research-it
This invaluable web site, already mentioned in Chapter 4, has links to translators to and from all the following languages: English, French, Danish, Spanish, Swedish, German, Italian, Turkish, Portuguese, Dutch, Russian, Czech, Slovenian, Romanian, Latvian, Serbian, Croatian, Polish, Greek, Chinese, Japanese, Latin and more. Research It! also has a language identifier. You enter a sentence of unknown origin and it identifies the language concerned. There is also a French verb conjugator.

Translating foreign web sites

While the majority of web sites are written in English, there are many in French, German, Spanish, Italian, Japanese and so on. When researching using the net, you are very likely to find sites relevant to your subject but in other languages. If 'O' level French or GCSE Spanish seem a long time ago, how will you get the most from these resources?

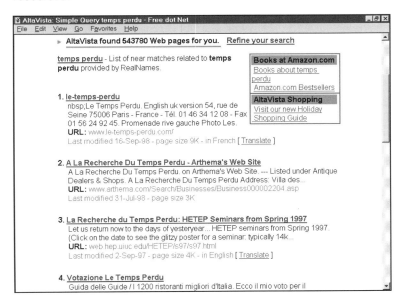

Fig. 54. AltaVista search results on 'temps perdu'.

Babel Fish translator...

Help is at hand in the form of the Babel Fish translator, which is provided in association with the search engine AltaVista. Let's say a search on AltaVista has produced one or more web sites in French. The example in Figure 54 used the search term 'temps perdu'.

Fig. 55. The Babel Fish translator dialog box.

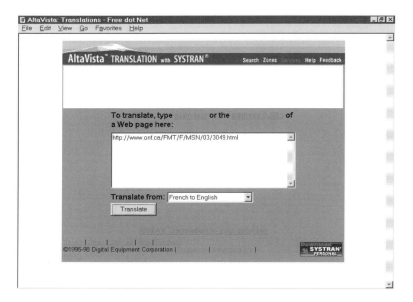

As you might expect, many of the web sites found by AltaVista are in French. However, you will notice that each listing has the word 'translate' in brackets after it. Clicking on this (it is a hyperlink) calls up the Babel Fish translator (Figure 55). As you will see, the web site URL is already displayed in the Babel Fish dialog box, so simply click on 'Translate' to see the site in question in a rough-and-ready English translation (Figure 56).

You do not have to search with AltaVista in order to use Babel Fish. To call it up directly, simply enter babelfish.altavista.digital.com in your browser's Open dialog box. You can then type or paste in a passage for translation, or enter the URL of any foreign language site of your choice.

Babel Fish is a handy free service, but its translations can be approximate, to say the least. If you need to translate foreign language web pages and other documents on a regular basis, it is well worth obtaining a translation program for your computer, such as Globalink Language Assistant.

Globalink Language Assistant

Globalink Language Assistant is one such translation program (see Figure 57). It can be found at:

www.globalink.com/pages/product-language-assistant.html

Globalink Language Assistant uses a form of artificial intelligence to analyse and translate text sentence by sentence, producing high quality draft translations.

Globalink Language Assistant is available in two versions. There is a 'Euro pack', which will translate documents to and from French, German and Italian, and a 'Latin pack', which translates to and from Spanish and Portuguese.

Language Assistant installs onto your computer's hard disk. It works as a stand-alone program, or will integrate with recent versions of Microsoft Word and Corel WordPerfect. As with AltaVista's Babel Fish, you can paste or type a document into the program, then select 'Translate' to have it translated. Language Assistant has a number of extra features as well.

1. You can use the program interactively to fine tune your translations.
2. You can personalise the program by adding new words to its dictionary.
3. You can print out line-by-line translations, with each translated line below its original counterpart.
4. You can also practise speaking the language of your choice, using the interactive language-learning lessons provided.

Fig. 56. Babel Fish translation of French web site

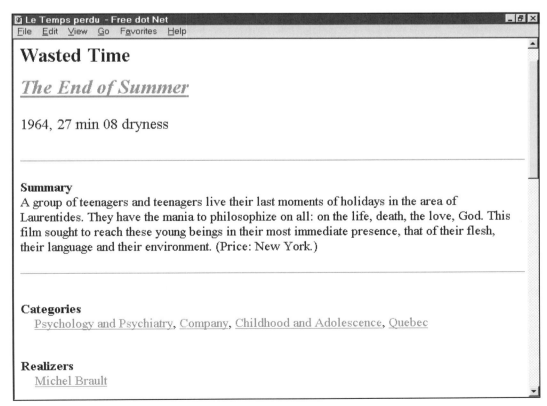

Le Temps perdu - Free dot Net

File   Edit   View   Go   Favorites   Help

Wasted Time

The End of Summer

1964, 27 min 08 dryness

Summary
A group of teenagers and teenagers live their last moments of holidays in the area of Laurentides. They have the mania to philosophize on all: on the life, death, the love, God. This film sought to reach these young beings in their most immediate presence, that of their flesh, their language and their environment. (Price: New York.)

Categories
   Psychology and Psychiatry, Company, Childhood and Adolescence, Quebec

Realizers
   Michel Brault

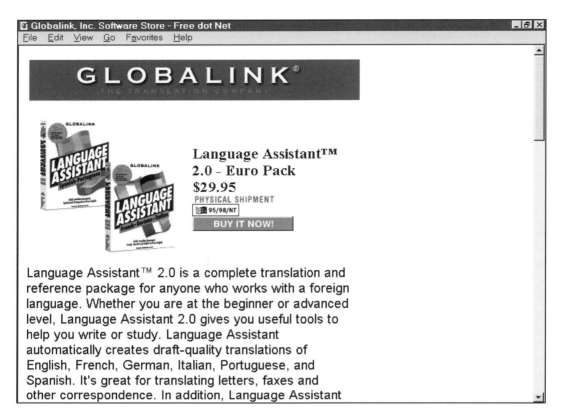

Fig. 57. The Globalink home page.

Globalink Language Assistant can be ordered online from the USA. It is also available in the UK from stores such as PC World. The price at the time of writing is around £30.

Pros and cons of computer translators

Pros
1. free or inexpensive
2. very fast
3. handy for draft translations
4. open up millions of non-English web sites

Cons
1. translations often too literal
2. idiomatic phrases do not translate well
3. some words not in dictionaries may be left untranslated
4. not really suitable for finished books or articles

How to use an online bookshop

In general the internet has been slow to take off as a retail medium. The big exception to this rule, however, has been online bookshops. Although purchases still have to be sent by the traditional post, the online medium lends itself very well to cataloguing books and to searching quickly for a particular author, title or subject area.

To see what an online bookshop can offer, point your browser at Amazon:

www.amazon.co.uk

This is the UK subsidiary of Amazon.com, the giant US-based online bookseller. The Amazon.com group is said to be the world's most visited internet retailer. On their site they claim to have more than 1.5 million customers in 160 countries around the world.

Amazon.co.uk is the UK's most popular internet bookstore (see Figure 58). Because they exist on the web they have unlimited 'shelf space' and can offer a selection of more than 1.4 million titles (compared with a typical physical world bookshop, which carries about 25,000 titles).

Finding the book you want

At an online bookshop you can search for books in a number of ways. First, like a traditional bookshop customer, you can simply browse through the categories and see what catches your eye. Various books are highlighted on the home page, and you can also see the current list of best-sellers (with full details) by clicking on the appropriate menu item at the top of the screen.

Let's suppose, however, that you want to see all the books available from the store by a particular author. In this case you would use the

Fig. 58. The Amazon.co.uk home page.

search facility at the top left of the screen. Say, for example, you want to get a list of all available books by the late American science fiction author Roger Zelazny. Enter his name in the dialog box, and click on 'Go' . . . And there you have a list of all Zelazny's available works (Figure 59).

Fig. 59. Amazon.co.uk author listing.

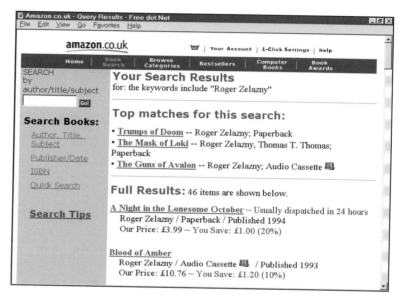

For each book you can click to see more information, check out readers' reviews, and author and publisher comments (assuming the latter are available). Figure 60, for example, shows the details for Zelazny's novel, *Nine Princes in Amber*.

Fig. 60. Example of the book details screen on Amazon.co.uk.

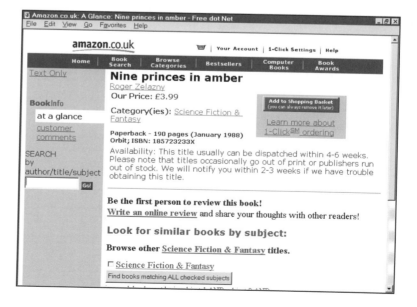

How to order

If you want to buy the above – or any other – book, the procedure at Amazon.co.uk is quite straightforward.

1. When you've found a book you want, click the button labelled *Add to shopping basket* to hold it until you are ready to buy it.

2. When you have identified all the books you want, click on the shopping basket icon at the top of the screen.

3. Next, click on the button marked *Proceed to Checkout.*

4. You now have to fill out a secure online order form, giving details such as your name and address, your credit card number and, of course, the books you want.

5. Click the button 'Press this to submit your order' and the transaction will be complete. Amazon.co.uk will send you an order confirmation by email.

Other online bookshops differ slightly in their methods, but generally they all use an ordering procedure similar to this one.

Promoting your book in an online bookshop

In a conventional bookshop you might have the opportunity to spend a day or half-day meeting readers and signing copies of your book. Internet bookshops allow you to do rather better than this.

For a start, both you and your publisher can attach commentaries about your book. Then, when anyone requests details about your title, they will be able to read what you have put. With a bit of luck, this may be just the incentive they need to add your book to their shopping list!

To find out which of your titles are stocked by Amazon.co.uk, enter your name in the search dialog box on the home page and click on *Go*. Click on each title, and at the bottom of the details page you will see the following options:

▷ I have read this book and I want to review it.

▷ I am the author and I want to comment on my book.

▷ I am the publisher and I want to comment on this book.

Click on the middle one of these and you can add your commentary for others to read. This need not merely be a paragraph or two. You are allowed to add book jacket images, reviews, excerpts, synopses, jacket copy ('blurb') and more.

This is not the only way you can promote your books at Amazon.co.uk. You can also post a 'self-interview' using the online form provided. This will appear with all your titles, and it is also available separately for browsing. The interview gives you a chance to tell readers about your influences and motivations for writing, working methods, future plans, and so on.

Finally, you can place a link on your web site to your title in Amazon.co.uk's database. Any sales from this, as well as generating the normal royalties for you, will also qualify you for a referral fee of up to 15 percent from Amazon. As well as generating extra revenue for you, this means that people browsing your site will have a quick and easy method of buying your book there and then. In effect you are adding secure ordering facilities to your home page, and there is no charge to you for participating.

Your questions answered

What other online bookshops are there?

UK-based stores include:

Waterstones	www.waterstones.co.uk
Bookstore	www.bookstore.co.uk
The Internet Bookshop	www.bookshop.co.uk

There are also many American bookshops, including:

Barnes & Noble	barnesandnoble.bfast.com
Amazon.com	www.amazon.com
Kingbooks.com	www.kingbooks.com

Can I save money by buying from the USA?

You may be able to. Prices are often slightly lower in the USA, but this must be set against the higher shipping charges and the probable longer wait to receive the books. Nevertheless, if you want to order a lot of books it is certainly worth investigating to see whether savings can be made.

Is there an easy way to check the best prices available on any book?

Various services will do this for you. One such is Acses:

www.acses.com

This site allows you to search for the book you want and check on prices and availability at any of 25 online bookstores (including all those mentioned above).

Are there any other benefits of using online bookshops?

New features are constantly being added. For example, at Amazon.-co.uk you can register your interests and receive free email notification of new books on these topics as they are published. The Amazon.com site includes a chart of the shop's top hundred best-sellers, updated hourly. Assuming you are in the lucky position of having written a US best-seller, you can sit and watch your book climbing up the charts!

Pros and cons of online bookshops

Pros

1. huge range of books in store
2. easy searching by author, title or subject
3. you can read reviews/commentaries before you buy
4. many books are sold at discount
5. opportunity to promote your work
6. growing range of additional features

Cons

1. have to wait days or weeks to receive books
2. extra charges for post and packing
3. can't physically browse the book before buying
4. not all titles carry reviews/commentaries

8 Working in Cyberspace

In this chapter you will discover how to:

▶ *combat viruses and hoaxes*
▶ *negotiate electronic reproduction rights*
▶ *avoid censorship and plagiarism*
▶ *negotiate contracts in cyberspace*

. . . .

How to combat viruses and hoaxes

Computer viruses are small programs concealed in apparently harm-less carriers such as programs, word processing documents and floppy disks. When you use an infected program, the virus transfers itself to your computer and starts copying itself to other programs, files or disks on your machine.

Apart from using up some of your computer's storage capacity, this might not be so bad. However, the really nasty aspect of viruses comes when they deliver their 'payload'. This is the effect which they are designed to produce. It may be anything from making a rude message appear on your screen, through deleting some files, to wiping your entire hard disk.

Over 18,000 computer viruses have been identified, though there are only a few hundred the average user is ever likely to encounter. Unfortunately, some of these are very widespread indeed. Computers can 'catch' viruses in various ways:

▷ from new software on a floppy disk or CD-ROM
▷ from the free cover disks on computer magazines
▷ from a friend's or colleague's floppy disk
▷ from a program or document attached to an email
▷ from some internet web sites and newsgroups

Types of virus

There are three main types of virus:

1. boot sector viruses
2. file viruses
3. macro viruses

Boot sector viruses

Boot sector viruses are the oldest. They work by replacing the special programming code which a computer reads when it 'boots up' (starts) with a different, virus-infected code. Boot sector viruses are usually passed on via floppy disks. If you accidentally leave an infected disk in the drive, when you next start your computer it will read the boot sector of the infected disk rather than the usual code on your hard disk. This will activate the virus, which will then infect the hard disk of your computer and any other disks you use.

File viruses

File viruses are sometimes called parasitic viruses. These viruses hide their code inside a program such as a word processor or computer game. Once a program is infected, every time it runs it becomes active in the computer's RAM (random access memory) and infects any other programs you run. If you pass a copy of an infected program to a friend, that copy will also be infected with the virus.

Macro viruses

Macro viruses are the most recent to appear. They can infect only certain office software packages, principally Microsoft Office (and especially Word). As the name suggests, these viruses are transmitted via macros: special mini-programs which run within programs such as Word. Macros perform a useful role by automating many routine functions. Unfortunately, though, programs which use them are susceptible to infection by viruses. Once a program has become infected by a macro virus, any document you work on in that program will become infected by the virus.

One very common Word macro virus is the **CAP** virus. Once your computer is infected with this, any document you try to save will be saved as a template instead of an ordinary document. What's more, any documents you send as email attachments or on floppy disk will be infected, and will pass the infection on to the recipient if he or she uses the same word processing program.

Virus precautions

Despite the periodic scare stories, if you use the internet sensibly you are unlikely to catch a virus from that source. There is a much higher relative risk from floppy disks, especially from unknown sources. To be safe, observe the following guidelines:

1. Avoid exchanging disks with friends or colleagues – including editors, publishers, proof readers, illustrators, and literary agents. If you do exchange disks, be sure to use a **virus checker** (see below) before running any program or opening any file.

2. Don't let your children put disks in your computer they have brought back from school. Schools and other educational institutions are among the most common sources of virus infections.

3. Take floppy disks out of your disk drive as soon as you have finished using them.

4. Use **Rich Text Format** (RTF) when exchanging word processing files. This will preserve most of your formatting, but cannot transmit viruses.

5. Avoid downloading software from non-reputable sources. Virus writers have been known to post samples of their work in programs downloadable from some of the seedier web sites and newsgroups.

6. Keep your floppy disks **write-protected** until you want to write to them.

7. Open Microsoft Word files from unknown sources using Quick View, WordPad or the Microsoft Word viewer, rather than Word itself.

8. Keep copies of all your files on floppy disks or some other storage device so that you can recover them if you become the victim of a virus. This is, in any event, good practice.

9. If you are using a recent version of Word, ensure that the *Macro Virus Protection* feature is enabled. You will find this under *Options* in the *Tools* menu.

10. Finally, install a modern virus checker on your computer and check every new program or file, no matter what its source, before running or opening it.

Virus checkers

Virus checkers are specialist programs you install on your computer's hard disk. In most cases they will then run quietly in the background. If they detect a virus, however, they will alert you and attempt to 'disinfect' the virus. You should also be able to virus check individual files (for example a program you have just downloaded from the internet) on demand.

The main virus checkers suitable for home users, with their company web pages and contact phone numbers, are as follows:

Dr Solomon's HomeGuard
www.drsolomon.com
Tel: (01296) 318700

Inoculan AntiVirus
www.cheyenne.com
Tel: (01737) 775500

Norton AntiVirus Deluxe
www.symantec.com
Tel: (0171) 616 5800

McAfee VirusScan
www.mcafee.com
Tel: (01753) 827500

PC-cillin
www.rmg.co.uk
Tel: (0181) 875 4444

Quarterdeck ViruSweep
www.quarterdeck.com
Tel: (0645) 123521

You can order virus checkers through the web pages listed above. They are also stocked by most computer retailers, for example PC World and Software Warehouse.

As new viruses appear all the time, virus checkers need regular updating. All the programs listed above can be updated via the internet. Your first year's updates (and possibly more) are generally included in the cost of the program.

Hoaxes

A direct result of the fear and confusion caused by viruses has been the appearance of email 'hoaxes'. These messages are written by people who think it would be amusing to cause panic by making people think they have a virus.

Most hoaxes warn the recipient of a terrifying new virus which is sent via email and will wipe their hard disk as soon as they open it. One of the best known hoaxes is 'Good Times'. In one of its many variations, this reads as follows:

> 'WARNING! There is a virus on America Online being sent by Email. If you get anything called "Good Times", DON'T read it or download it. It is a virus that will erase your hard drive. Forward this to all your friends. It may help them a lot.'

There is a host of variations on this theme. Other equally apocalyptic emails warn of mythical viruses in messages headed 'Penpal Greetings', 'Returned or Unable to Deliver' and 'Win a Holiday'. Other hoax warnings refer to viruses in programs called AOL4FREE, PKZ300B and a 'highly desirable' screensaver called Budweiser Frogs.

All of the above are hoaxes and should be ignored. It is impossible to contract a virus simply by reading an email as these messages claim. A virus can, of course, be passed on by a program sent as an attachment to an email; so it is important to run a virus checker over any such file from an unknown source before opening or running it. But, to repeat the main point once again, plain internet emails *cannot* transmit viruses.

Negotiating your rights..

Your questions answered

Why do people write viruses?

For a variety of reasons. Some enjoy the intellectual challenge. Others feel they have a point to make about society's growing dependence on computers. Others are bored, resentful about their jobs, or just plain anti-social. Whatever the reasons, there are newsgroups and mailing lists devoted to virus writing if you know where to look, so they are likely to be around for a long time to come.

How can I find out more about viruses and hoaxes?

For general questions and answers, try the newsgroup:

comp.virus

There are also many web sites with more information. Start by reading the Computer Virus FAQ at:

www.datafellows.fi/vl-faq.htm#A7

For information about hoaxes, see the Good Times Virus Hoax FAQ at:

www.hr.doe.gov/goodtime.html

I've just had a message from Bill Gates promising me £1,000 if I forward copies of it to all my friends. Is it genuine?

No! This is another hoax. These type of messages are variations on the old chain letter principle. If you get any messages asking you to forward emails, money or get-well cards to other people, simply delete them. Do not pass them on.

An author's guide to negotiating electronic reproduction rights

The internet and other electronic media, such as publishing on floppy disk and CD-ROM, have created a host of new opportunities for writers. Unfortunately they have also created something of a battleground as traditional publishers have attempted to persuade authors to sign away their rights in the new media. It is therefore worth recapping on what your rights as a UK-based author are.

1. As a freelance, anything you create, you own. It doesn't matter whether this is a novel, a non-fiction book, an article, a short story or a reader's letter. If you are working as an employee, on the other hand, ownership in anything you produce belongs to your employer.

2. What you own is the actual arrangement of words on the page. There is no copyright on facts or ideas; so even if a producer or an editor suggested the original idea for your work, this does not affect your ownership of the finished work.

3. You can sell whatever rights you wish in your writing. Traditionally, writers sell limited reproduction rights to publishers, while still retaining ownership of their work. With articles, for example, it is customary to offer First British Serial Rights (FBSR), First North American Serial Rights (FNASR), and so on. Such a transaction allows the publisher to reproduce your work once in the area concerned, and leaves you free to sell other rights (for example Second British Serial Rights) as and when you can.

In recent years, there has been a trend for publishers to ask authors to 'assign' rights to them, often for no additional payment or (at best) a token fee. This means the publishers get unlimited rights to use your work as they see fit. This is sometimes expressed as signing over the copyright or 'all rights'. The effect is the same, however – by agreeing, you sign away your right to benefit in any way from future sales of your work.

The reason publishers are increasingly keen on authors assigning their rights to them is not hard to see. The electronic media open up whole new areas for them to exploit. Although sales are still relatively low, they can be expected to grow rapidly as more people obtain computers and get online.

For their part, publishers argue that there are practical difficulties in administering electronic rights payments. Rather than having to administer large numbers of small payments for such rights, they say, it is simpler and more cost-effective for them to obtain all rights from the start.

Negotiating with publishers

Needless to say, writers need to resist any pressure to assign all rights to publishers, and should challenge any such terms in their contracts. The argument about the difficulty of monitoring and calculating royalties due on electronic publications is weak at best. Software which can accurately measure (say) the number of 'hits' on a web site is now widely available. It is therefore just as easy for a publisher to work out royalties due on an electronic publication as would be the case with traditional book sales. When negotiating electronic rights, therefore, follow the guidelines below.

▷ Resist any attempt by a publisher or editor to make you 'assign' all rights.

▷ Insist that electronic rights should be negotiated separately, and included as a separate item in any publishing contract.

▷ Where publishers resist such a request, contact organisations such as the National Union of Journalists, the Writers Guild and The Society of Authors. Even if you are not a member of one of these organisations, they are all keen to ensure that authors are treated fairly over electronic rights, and may offer you practical advice and support.

Authors' rights ....

Your questions answered

My publisher claims that by cashing his cheque I have automatically accepted his terms. Is this correct?
This is not normally true, though it has not stopped some publishers and broadcasters from saying it. Under British law, cashing a cheque generally has no effect other than adding to your bank balance. Legally, to assign any rights you must agree to this, preferably in writing. However, personal circumstances will vary and if you are in any way concerned you should take professional legal advice.

What are 'moral rights', and do I still have them on the internet?
Moral rights are the right to a by-line or credit, and the right to object to the distortion of your work. In British law, moral rights do not apply to work which reports news and current affairs; and it is unclear whether they apply to features. You do have moral rights in fiction or non-fiction books, and these apply in all media, including electronic ones.

Do I need to get copyright permission before including links to other sites on my web page?
Almost certainly (until a court case settles this issue definitively) the answer is no. However, it is a courtesy to inform any such site that you would like to include a link to them.

What is 'fair use'?
'Fair use' is an exception to the general rule of copyright. It means you are allowed to copy short extracts from a copyright-protected work for certain purposes (principally, but not exclusively, review and scholarship), as long as the original source is credited. The law surrounding fair use is complex; but as a general principle, if you intend to copy more than a short paragraph from any copyright work, you should seek the copyright-holder's permission first.

Censorship and plagiarism

The internet has created a range of issues for legislators and ordinary citizens to ponder. High among these are issues surrounding censorship and privacy.

One major concern among parents and educators has been that through the net children will gain unrestricted access to hardcore pornography and other undesirable material.

As far as pornography is concerned, software packages such as Net Nanny provide a partial, if not a complete, solution. These programs work by looking for keywords such as 'sex', and deny the user access to sites containing these words. You can obtain Net Nanny at:

www.netnanny.com

Other areas such as information about drugs and weapons, racist material and so on are more difficult to block out. For this reason, some people have demanded that the net should be censored in a similar way to TV and other media. Leaving aside the practical question of how this could be accomplished, it is worth examining the pros and cons.

Pros and cons of censorship

Pros

1. reduces chances of undesirable material being seen by minors and other vulnerable individuals

2. less opportunity for the net to be used for criminal purposes

3. more control over who has access to sensitive (e.g. health-related) information

4. greater acceptance of the internet in schools and society generally

Cons

1. less opportunity for free debate on difficult and important issues

2. denies adults the freedom to make decisions for themselves

3. easier for governments to control access to information they dislike

4. who will decide what is acceptable or unacceptable for the rest of us to see?

There are, of course, arguments for and against censorship. However, there is also the question of how it could be implemented. The internet transcends traditional national boundaries; so the rulings of a censorship authority in the UK would have no influence over a web site originating in (say) Australia or the USA.

The alternative would be for IAPs to stop users in the UK accessing 'banned' sites. Through a voluntary agreement between IAPs this already happens to some extent. However, the sheer size of the internet, and the rate at which it is growing and changing, makes it unlikely that this method of censorship could ever be 100% effective.

Many writers (including the present author), while sympathising with the concerns of the pro-censorship lobby, place a high value on the freedom of information on the net. For this reason, rather than favouring censorship, they believe that people should be taught and encouraged to use the wealth of material on the net selectively and intelligently.

Censorship issues

Privacy and censorship is an area of rapid change, and any book purporting to provide a definitive review of the legal position would be out of date as soon as it was written. Instead, here are a number of real-

Legal questions raised by censorship ....

life cases illustrating the issues and problems affecting writers which are occurring at the moment. All of these are genuine news stories which occurred during the time this book was being written.

▷ A journalist travelling from Paris to London's Waterloo Station was stopped by two customs officers. One officer asked whether he had net access on his laptop computer, to which he replied yes. She then asked if he had pornography on it, to which he replied no. The officer said she would have to scan the computer's hard disk to check he was not lying. This she proceeded to do. Is this a justifiable procedure for controlling the import of banned materials, or an infringement of personal liberty? How would you feel if it happened to you?

▷ Police chiefs in the UK have been in secret talks with internet access providers over proposals to allow the police access to private emails. The police want the right to read messages on submission of a standard form, signed by an officer of super-intendent rank or higher, to the internet access provider concerned. The IAPs are unhappy with the proposals, but feel they will have no choice but to comply or risk having their assets seized. Is this a necessary measure to allow the police to get on with their jobs unhindered by red tape? Or is it simply a ploy to extend the police's powers of search without having to obtain the permission of a court? How would you feel about the police being free to read all your letters in the Post Office?

▷ Two Scottish newspapers have been involved in a bitter legal dispute over their web sites. The *Shetland Times* objected to its web-only rival the *Shetland News* including hyperlinks to stories on its web site. The court granted the *Shetland Times* an interim interdict (injunction) forbidding the *Shetland News* from including links to the *Times*. The case was eventually settled out of court. The *News* was allowed to include links to stories in its rival, as long as there was a clear acknowledgement that the link was to a *Times* story, and in each case a link was also provided to the *Times* headlines page. What (if any) would have been the implications for internet users in Scotland had the *Shetland Times* won its case in court?

▷ The Government is currently considering proposals to introduce a **key escrow** system in the UK. This means that any provider of data encryption technology (the programs which permit secure transac-tions over the internet) would have to supply to an independent agency a copy of the codes used to encrypt data. Anyone would then be free to approach this agency and, as long as they could provide a convincing reason, obtain a key enabling them to read private emails and other encrypted information (e.g. credit card numbers). Are these proposals justifiable as an attempt to counter criminal activities – or another move towards a 'Big Brother' state where privacy is unobtainable? The following rhyme was found on the internet:

Little Mary had a key:
She put it in escrow,
And everything that Mary did
The Feds were bound to know.

Keeping up to date with censorship

As you might expect, the internet is well supplied with sites covering privacy and censorship issues. Useful web sites include the following.

The Copyright Website
www.benedict.com
An American site giving a lot of useful information about copyright issues in a very readable style.

Cyber-Rights and Cyber-Liberties
www.leeds.ac.uk/law/pgs/yaman/ukpriva.htm
Includes useful information on encryption systems and the current debate about key escrow.

Electronic Frontier Foundation
www.eff.org/pub/Privacy/HTML/hot.html
The 'What's hot in privacy' bulletins are a good way of keeping up with the latest issues.

Electronic Privacy Information Centre
www.epic.org
EPIC is a campaigning organisation based in Washington DC. The site includes many useful articles on privacy and censorship issues.

National Union of Journalists
www.gn.apc.org/media/nuj.html
The NUJ web site includes a number of useful articles about copyright issues.

Privacy International UK
www.privacy.org/pi/countries/uk
The UK section of the Privacy Site, looking at UK privacy issues from a global perspective.

The Privacy Site
www.privacy.org
A huge site including information on privacy issues of all kinds (not just internet-related) throughout the world.

Mailing list

The American Society of Journalists and Authors (ASJA) produces a regular Contracts Watch briefing. This is available to non-members as an internet mailing list. To subscribe, send an email with the text SUBSCRIBE ASJACW-L to the address:

majordomo@eskimo.com

Copyright matters. . . . .

Briefings are sent roughly every month. Contracts Watch also carries some UK news via the NUJ's London freelance branch bulletin, the *Freelance*.

Newsgroups

The following very lively newsgroups cover privacy and censorship issues:

alt.censorship	news.admin.censorship
alt.security	sci.crypt
comp.risks	talk.politics.crypto
comp.security	uk.politics.censorship

Plagiarism

Plagiarism, of course, refers to the wholesale copying of another author's work. Unfortunately, anything published electronically is especially vulnerable to this. As many teachers are well aware, it takes only a few seconds to copy an article from a web page or CD-ROM and paste it into your own work.

The legal position in the UK of material published electronically is clear. Like all original creative work in a tangible form, it enjoys full copyright protection under UK law. There is no need to 'register' your work to 'obtain' copyright. However, the trans-national nature of the net can make it difficult to enforce your rights. For example, a UK court ruling in your favour is unlikely to be much help if the web site infringing your copyright is based in (say) Venezuela.

Of course, some plagiarism is committed by people who simply do not realise that by doing so they are breaking the law. It is therefore a good idea to put on your web home page a copyright statement. The one below is an example you might like to adapt:

> Copyright Notice
>
> The information on this web site is provided for the benefit of the general online community. All text and images remain the property of the copyright-holder, Jayne Writer. The site may not be reproduced wholly or in part, by any means whatsoever, including 'mirroring' on other web-servers, without prior written consent of the author. Printing out sections for personal use and storing them on your computer are permitted. Linking to this site is encouraged; notifying me is appreciated.
>
> Copyright 1998; Jayne Writer, Anytown, Middleshire.

If your site includes material which could be useful for teachers, you might like to add an extra line, for example:

'Teachers may reproduce sections from this site for classroom use, as long as the original source is clearly indicated.'

Educational writers might find this a good way of promoting their books, as long as they do not give away too much free!

Adding a copyright notice to your site will be generally appreciated by those people (the majority of internet users) who wish to abide by the rules and respect the rights of writers and other creative artists.

Contracts in cyberspace

The internet has added a new level of complexity to negotiating contracts. While it is impossible to give definitive advice in a fast-changing world, the following are points to bear in mind:

1. As yet, there is no form of electronic signature which is acceptable in a UK court of law. To create a binding contract, you are still likely to need a written document signed by both parties.

2. When signing a contract with a web-based publisher, remember that any dispute will normally have to be settled under the laws of the country in which the publisher is based. If you are unhappy about this, you may be able to negotiate an additional clause that any dispute should be settled under the legal system of England and Wales.

3. With internet emails, there is no way to prove conclusively whether or not someone has received your message. If you need 'proof positive' that an email has been received, therefore, you should always request a written acknowledgement.

4. As previously mentioned, never agree to assign all rights. Ensure that any contract you sign, even with a conventional publisher, includes a separate clause on electronic rights. As well as Internet rights, these might include publishing on floppy disk, CD-ROM, DVD (digital video disk), laser disk, computer game rights and so on. Your future earnings from such sources may be considerable.

5. Even where a publisher is not charging for work published electronically, he may still be profiting from it. Several conventionally published magazines raised their advertising rates when they opened web sites, on the basis that they were now reaching a much wider audience via the net. There is no reason why writers should not receive a share of these extra profits.

6. Ensure that you retain your self-employed status. If the law regards you as an employee, you will have no rights in any of the work you produce for your client. If you have to prove your self-employed status, it will help if you can meet as many as possible of the following criteria:

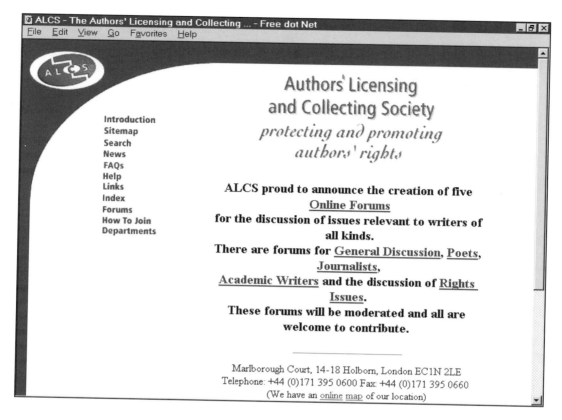

Authors' Licensing
and Collecting Society
*protecting and promoting
authors' rights*

Introduction
Sitemap
Search
News
FAQs
Help
Links
Index
Forums
How To Join
Departments

ALCS proud to announce the creation of five
Online Forums
for the discussion of issues relevant to writers of
all kinds.
There are forums for General Discussion, Poets,
Journalists,
Academic Writers and the discussion of Rights
Issues.
These forums will be moderated and all are
welcome to contribute.

Marlborough Court, 14-18 Holborn, London EC1N 2LE
Telephone: +44 (0)171 395 0600 Fax: +44 (0)171 395 0660
(We have an online map of our location)

Fig. 61. The ALCS
home page.

(a) you work for more than one client

(b) you work mainly from your own home or office

(c) you have day-to-day control over how you organise your work

(d) you invoice your clients for work completed.

7. Remember that cyberspace is very much the new frontier, and many legal issues surrounding it are still unclear. The only way to keep up to date is to read the newspapers, visit web sites such as those listed earlier in this chapter, and subscribe to relevant newsgroups and mailing lists. In cases of difficulty, writers' organisations such as the Society of Authors may be able to provide advice and support.

The Authors' Licensing and Copyright Society

Finally, a word must be said about the Authors' Licensing and Copyright Society (ALCS):

www.alcs.co.uk

This UK organisation works on behalf of writers to ensure that they benefit fully from their creative work. In particular, ALCS administers a range of rights which are best handled collectively. These include:

▷ reprography (photocopying)

▷ lending

.... **Authors' Licensing and Copyright Society**

▷ electronic rights
▷ some broadcast rights
▷ cable re-transmission
▷ private recording
▷ off-air recording
▷ public reception of broadcasts
▷ rental

ALCS administers rights in Great Britain and Northern Ireland. It also covers other territories (e.g. Germany) through reciprocal arrangements with collecting societies there. Fees are collected from users of copyright work such as colleges and universities, and distributed quarterly in February, May, August and November. The annual distribution currently amounts to over £10 million.

ALCS is involved in a range of other activities. It keeps a watching brief on all matters affecting copyright in the UK and abroad, and makes representations to the UK government and European Union. It is active in the field of electronic rights and produces a range of publications on this subject. ALCS has also launched a world-wide syndication service called ByLine for articles written by its members. There is a separate web site for this:

www.universalbyline.co.uk.

Members of the Writers' Guild and the Society of Authors receive ALCS membership free of charge. Others can join the organisation and support its work for a small annual fee (£5.88 including VAT at the time of writing). You do not, however, have to be a member of ALCS to benefit from the funds distributed.

9 Web sites for writers

This chapter, which is somewhat different from the preceding ones, lists a large number of web sites which may be of interest to writers. They are divided into four main categories:

▶ *general writing sites*
▶ *reference resources*
▶ *publishers*
▶ *sites by and about writers*

GENERAL WRITING SITES

Adobe Magazine

www.adobemag.com

This is an online archive of articles from Adobe's magazine about desktop publishing. The articles are searchable by title, subject or date. You will need Adobe Acrobat Reader (downloadable free of charge from the site) in order to view the articles.

Alternet

www.alternet.org/

This 'alternative' news service syndicates articles from a variety of non-mainstream US newspapers and magazines. An especially useful section for journalists is 'Steal This Story' in the News You Can Use section. This provides articles which can be adapted for your local area and readership. Most of the site is free, but you have to become a member to search the archives and to download the complete text of some stories. AlterNet also advertises job vacancies in non-profit media.

Aspiring Writer

www.connet80.com/-aspire/New_aspire/index.html

This online magazine is aimed at new and established writers. It includes a chat room where you can communicate in real time with other writers, and editors who are willing to review your manuscripts. There are also cartoons to cheer you up when the writing isn't flowing.

Authorlink!

www.authorlink.com

This extensive news, information and marketing site is dedicated to authors, literary agents and publishers. Among the many features are news about developments in the US publishing industry, market information, tips for writers, interviews with editors and publishers, classified job advertisements, competitions, and more. Authorlink! also includes a showcase service, whereby authors can (for a fee) have their manuscripts evaluated and previewed on the site, in the hope of catching the eye of agents and publishers.

Authors' Licensing and Copyright Society (ALCS)

www.alcs.co.uk

This is the web site of the Authors' Licensing and Copyright Society. This UK organisation works on behalf of writers to ensure that they benefit fully from their creative work. It administers a range of rights which are best handled collectively, including photocopying, off-air recording and electronic rights. The site includes information on ALCS's history and its work today, and includes online forms for registering your work with them.

Author's Showcase

www.light-communications.com/author/index.html

This site describes itself as 'an online bookstore of published and self-published authors who showcase their books with pictures, sample text, and ordering information.' For an annual fee of around $400 they will create a page for your book and, they claim, market it actively to readers, agents and publishers.

Authors Speak

www.authorsspeak.com

This site uses Real Audio technology to broadcast recorded interviews with modern writers. You will therefore need a multimedia computer with speakers and a suitable soundcard in order to benefit from it. The interviews are hosted by Henry L.Tischler, a professor of sociology and regular radio broadcaster. The site includes one-to-one interviews with writers such as beat poet Allen Ginsberg, humorist Dave Barry, and author Whitley Strieber.

Black Star Press

www.blackstarpress.com/

Black Star Press is a poetry publisher, but their site also includes chat rooms, writers' forums, an online bookshop, a calendar of literary events, and a page of links to other writing-related sites.

Bricolage

bricolage.bel-epa.com/

Bricolage is a well established, UK-based electronic magazine for writers, albeit one that appears at irregular intervals. Among the contents is a useful, though small, selection of articles for beginning writers, and a range of market information (mainly books, magazines and electronic publications) not easily available elsewhere.

Children's Writing Resource Centre

www.mindspring.com/~cbi/

This is a site aimed at people who write children's literature or would like to. It includes information about new publications, best-selling children's authors, children's book publishers and other useful information for writers in this field. The site includes monthly articles on writing for children, and FAQs covering various topics in this area.

Web sites for writers ....

There is also a guide to finding a publisher, and a page of tips for beginners.

Committee to Protect Journalists
www.cpj.org
As the name suggests, this site and the organisation behind it are concerned with protecting press freedom. The committee monitors and reports on attacks on journalists, and lists cases where they have been threatened, illegally detained or imprisoned. The site includes CPJ press releases, and issues of the organisation's newsletter *Dangerous Assignments Quarterly*. Special reports are available on subjects such as 'Homophobic Attacks on the Press'. The site can also be searched by key words.

Computer Book Cafe
www.studiob.com
The Computer Book Cafe is sponsored by StudioB, a literary agency for computer book authors. The site includes articles about the computer book industry, lists of publishers, financial information, and so on. There is a free mailing list you can subscribe to. The site also includes information about the StudioB agency and how to become represented by them.

Creators' Copyright Coalition
www.gn.apc.org/media/cccindex.html
The UK Creators' Copyright Coalition (CCC) was formed on 20th March 1995 to defend freelance rights against their attempted erosion by several UK publishers. The web site includes a statement of the coalition's aims, information about the progress of its campaigning, and a list of affiliated organisations, with hyperlinks where available.

Drew's Scripts-o-Rama
www.script-o-rama.com
Describing itself as 'the most comprehensive index of movie and television scripts available on the Internet', this site includes links to TV and film scripts which can be downloaded from the net. Some of these are simply transcripts of films and TV programmes, but others are the actual scripts used, including shooting scripts and early drafts.

Eclectic Writer
www.eclectics.com/writing/writing.html
The Eclectic Writer is a neatly presented site with a bias towards fiction writing. It includes a selection of articles, for example 'How to Write a Sensual Romance' and 'The Perfect Query Letter'. There are also links to sites of interest to writers, divided into categories.

Elements of Style
www.cc.columbia.edu/acis/bartleby/strunk/
For many years *The Elements of Style* by Strunk and White has been a standard text in schools and colleges. A no-nonsense guide to grammar, punctuation, word choice and so on, it has been through

many reprints and editions. The original 1918 version is now out of copyright, however, and available via various web sites. While some may think it old-fashioned, many more consider it an essential guide to the basics of the writing craft.

Eleven Rules of Grammar

www.mailzone.com/users/pub/rgiaquinta/writing.shtml

This site provides a concise guide to some of the main rules of grammar; for example, 'Use the active voice unless you specifically need to use the passive'. One or two of the rules may appear a bit prescriptive for UK tastes; for example one rule states that an introductory phrase should *always* be offset by a comma. Samples of correct and incorrect usage are given, together with online and hard copy references. Links to other grammar and writing resources on the web are provided.

Essays on the Craft of Dramatic Writing

www.teleport.com/~bjscript/index.htm

This site includes a collection of essays on dramatic writing mainly for TV and film. The essays are by the site's creator, Bill Johnson (author of *A Story is a Promise*). Titles include 'Foundation principles of story-telling', 'Writing a story synopsis' and 'Creating story characters'. The site also includes reviews of films in the context of their screenplays, resources for film and television writers, and script requests from a number of North American TV and film producers and theatre companies, by courtesy of the Northwest Playwrights Guild.

Gender-Free Pronoun FAQ

www.eecis.udel.edu/~chao/gfp/

Sooner or later, every writer has to grapple with the problem of what to do about the English language's lack of a singular third-person gender-free pronoun. Writing *he/she* all the time looks clumsy, *he* on its own invites accusations of sexism, and *they* as a singular pronoun is ungrammatical. The authors of this site look at the history of the problem, examine how past and present writers have found ways around it, and suggest some solutions (which may not be to everyone's taste) of their own.

Grammar and Style Notes

www.english.upenn.edu/~jlynch/Grammar/

Grammar and Style Notes is organised alphabetically. There are two main subject areas: specific usage articles (for example, *it's* versus *its*), and articles on more general stylistic points. The text is clearly written, with plenty of examples of correct and incorrect usage to underline the points made. Links are included to other grammatical reference sites on the web.

Grammar Queen

www.grammarqueen.com

The Grammar Queen dispenses free advice on grammatical matters to anyone writing in. The site also includes articles on grammar, spelling and punctuation, and links to other grammar-related sites.

Guide to Grammar and Writing

webster.commnet.edu/HP/pages/darling/grammar.htm

This invaluable site is produced by Professor Charles Darling at the Capital Community Technical College in Connecticut. If you want to find out the difference between a dependent and an independent clause, or how to avoid a dangling modifier, this is the place to come. The site includes a number of interactive tests and quizzes, all with instant feedback. There is also a free 'Ask Grammar' service for any questions you may have on grammar, punctuation, and so on.

HorrorNet

www.horrornet.com

HorrorNet aims to provide a comprehensive web site for readers and writers of horror and suspense fiction. It includes horror fiction and articles about the genre, publishing news, lists of events, interviews with writers, message boards and live chat forums. There are also hundreds of links to author sites, publisher sites, bookstores, multi-media, author email addresses, online fiction, magazines, and more.

Hypertext Resources on the Web

www.eastgate.com/Hypertext.html

This site is sponsored by Eastgate Systems, Inc., a leading producer of hypertext software. It provides a range of information for anyone who may be interested in creating hypertext fiction. This is fiction published electronically, mainly on the web or CD-ROM. Through the use of hypertext links, it allows reader interaction, image maps, sound and video links, online glossaries and explanations, stories with many possible branches and endings, and so on. As well as advice and articles, the site includes links to many examples of hypertext work.

Inklings Web Page

www.inkspot.com/inklings

Inklings is a free email newsletter for writers of all persuasions, fiction and non-fiction. Each fortnightly issue includes news and market information, and two or three short articles. The web site (see also below) includes a copy of the current issue and information on how you can subscribe.

Inkspot

www.inkspot.com

Inkspot is one of the top sites on the web for writing news and information. It includes market information, articles about the craft of writing, interviews with published writers, classified advertisements, writers' forums, and much more. The site also published the Inklings email newsletter (see above), and has an archive of back issues.

The Inner Circle Writers Club

www.geocities.com/circlefaq.htm

This is a free club for fiction writers from around the world. Through the club you can share writing tips and techniques, check your research with people who know first-hand, and exchange manuscripts for critiques. The group has around 1,500 members, many of whom enjoy appraising other members' work. If you wish to join The Inner Circle, you have to fill in a questionnaire. The information is then placed online on the club's profile pages, accessible to members only. Using the membership list, you will be able to find other writers of similar age, writing interests, and reading preferences as yourself. It is then open to you to write to these members asking them if they will appraise your work (and they, of course, can ask you to do likewise).

Institute for Alternative Journalism

www.igc.org/an/

If you want to dig out the less sensational but still important stories that are often overlooked by the mainstream media, this American site is well worth a visit. It includes links to independent news sources such as Democracy Works and the Media and Democracy Congress, as well as information about the IAJ itself. One potentially very useful resource on this site is the Expert Rolodex, a directory of expert contacts in North America in fields ranging from consumer law to gay and lesbian rights.

Investigative Journalism on the Internet

www.vir.com/~sher/julian.htm

Investigative Journalism on the Net is a comprehensive reference guide geared to the needs of the busy reporter. The Quick Story Tips section suggests the best places to start researching a story on the net. The Story Topics page includes dozens of leads for topics such as the environment, health, justice, women's rights, racism and so on. Media Indexes is a guide to mailing lists relevant to journalists, while Newspapers On Line lets you browse newspaper headlines from around the world.

Journalism Education Association

www.jea.org

The JEA is an international organisation of journalists, journalism teachers and other media professionals. It aims to 'make a permanent contribution to the dignity of the journalistic profession'. The web site includes curriculum guides and teaching materials and a list of publications for sale. Journalists' calendars and lists of forthcoming conferences are also posted here.

Journalism UK

www.octopod.demon.co.uk/journ_uk.htm

Journalism UK is a resource intended primarily for UK-based journalists working on text-based publications. It is a collection of links to sites of interest arranged in twelve categories: UK news, local news, magazines, e-zines, sources, jobs, recreation, TV and films, new books, organisations, world, sport, science, and 'this week'.

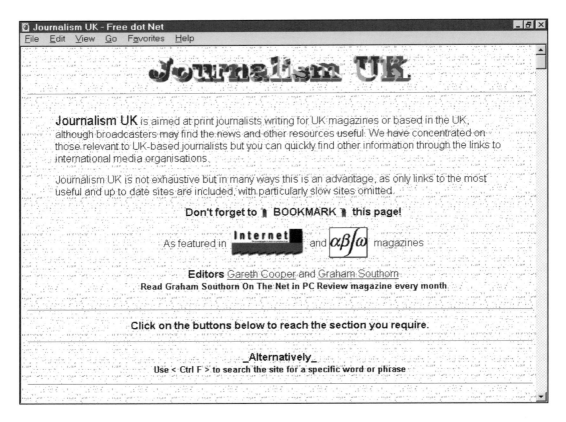

Journalism UK

Journalism UK is aimed at print journalists writing for UK magazines or based in the UK, although broadcasters may find the news and other resources useful. We have concentrated on those relevant to UK-based journalists but you can quickly find other information through the links to international media organisations.

Journalism UK is not exhaustive but in many ways this is an advantage, as only links to the most useful and up to date sites are included, with particularly slow sites omitted.

Don't forget to ▮ BOOKMARK ▮ this page!

As featured in **Internet** and $\alpha\beta\int\omega$ magazines

Editors Gareth Cooper and Graham Southorn
Read Graham Southorn On The Net in PC Review magazine every month.

Click on the buttons below to reach the section you require.

Alternatively
Use < Ctrl F > to search the site for a specific word or phrase

Fig. 62. The Journalism UK home page.

Lichfield & District Writers
www.philfr.demon.co.uk/
This is the web page of the Lichfield & District Writers. It will obviously be of most interest if you live near Lichfield in Staffordshire, but there are also details of the group's annual short story competition which is open to everyone.

Lydbury English Centre
www.edunet.com/clinic-h.html
This UK-based site includes articles on various aspects of writing and English usage. There is also a lively message board on which grammatical questions are asked and answered.

Market List
www.greyware.com/marketlist/
The Market List is a free resource for writers of SF, fantasy and horror. It includes articles, reviews, interviews and - of course - market information for writers in these genres. Links to other Web sites and earlier, archived versions of the list are provided.

Mystery Opportunities
www.slip.net/~cluelass/Opportunity.html
As the name suggests, this site publishes market information of interest to mystery writers, from beginners to published professionals. There are details of awards and competitions, calls for submissions, and advertisements from publishers requiring writers.

National Press Club

npc.press.org

The National Press Club is based in Washington, DC. Its web site brings a wide range of services and information to journalists across the world. Here you can access speeches from the NPC Luncheon series dating from 1990; these are available as audio files as long as you have the necessary technology to support them. The site also includes the NPC's Directory of News Sources. This is a huge list of contacts who should be able to assist you with any story you may be assigned.

National Union of Journalists

www.gn.apc.org/media/nuj.html

The NUJ is the world's largest journalists' union, with over 25,000 members in England, Scotland, Wales and Ireland. Their web site includes articles on such subjects as copyright, moral rights and the impact of digital technology; the NUJ campaign on digitally manipulated photographs; and why contracts are important, when they're not and how to negotiate them. Other features include information on journalistic training and qualifications, and the Union's online *Freelance* newsletter.

Novel Advice Newsletter

www.noveladvice.com

This free fortnightly newsletter has a fiction-writing bias, but a far wider scope than just novel writing. The full text of current and past issues is available on the site, and you can also have copies emailed to you by filling in a reply form.

One Day in the Life of an Albany Reporter

www.nylink.org/newsroom/daylife/

Essential viewing for anyone wanting a behind-the-scenes look at news journalism, this site features a day in the life of US reporter Victor Schaffner. You follow Victor as he goes through his day, checking out stories in rival papers, attending press conferences, sorting through press releases, and so on. The site is a kind of annotated electronic diary. The impressive multimedia effects mean you feel as though you are right there with Victor in the Albany newsroom. You will, however, need a modern browser with sound card and audio software to get the full effect.

Online Magazine Article Writing Workshop

www.freelanceworkshop.com

This commercial site hosted by Deadline Communications promotes their 'Writing for Publication' book and video and the associated online training course. You can see a six-minute video preview of the course, and enrol or order course material online. You can also visit the 'participant lounge' (chat room) and sample the discussions among past and present students on the course.

Web sites for writers ....

Online Writing Centers and Other Resources

wilmot.unh.edu/~arm1/wrcenter.html

This is a comprehensive list of online writing centres (note the American spelling in the title). Links to other sites of interest to writers are also included.

The Online Writery

www.missouri.edu/~wleric/writery.html

The Online Writery is based at the University of Missouri-Columbia. The site is intended to provide a forum for writers to interact with others of like mind. As well as various discussion forums, the site includes ZooMOO, a text-based chat area which enables writers to communicate with one another in real time. There is also an email discussion list you can subscribe to.

Poems on the Underground

www.netpoems.com/

Launched in 1986, Poems on the Underground was a project designed to give travellers on London's tube trains a moment's reflection, through the medium of short poems reproduced on posters. Many of the poems which have been published during the life of the project are accessible from this web site.

Poets and Writers Online

www.pw.org

This large, New York based site includes articles on various aspects of writing, panel discussions, forums, and much more. The Job Bank section lists writing jobs and calls for submissions for books, anthologies, magazines and so on. At the time of writing, article subjects included fifteen women writers whose cultural influences have spanned the globe, the secret of getting published, the art of reading a book contract, and a look at the future of publishing. The latter included links to over 70 web sites useful to writers. See Figure 63.

Purdue Online Writing Lab

owl.english.purdue.edu

This well organised and regularly updated site has become a model for similar 'writing laboratories' on the web. As well as discussion forums and samples of students' writing, the site includes a communally-generated style and usage manual.

Pure Fiction

www.purefiction.com

This growing site for fiction readers and writers is updated regularly. It includes competitions, articles about writing and writers, author interviews, lists of publishers and agents, internet links and more. The site is run jointly between the UK and the USA.

Rensselaer Writing Center

www.rpi.edu/web/writingcenter/

The Rensselaer Writing Center is located at the Rensselaer Polytechnic

Fig. 63. Poets and Writers Online home page.

Institute in Troy, New York. The site includes guidance sheets, aimed primarily at students, on topics such as revising prose and writing with gender-fair language. There is also a selection of links to online dictionaries and editing resources such as *Bartlett's Familiar Quotations* and *The Hacker's Dictionary of Computer Jargon.*

Reporter.org

www.reporter.org

If you need up-to-the-minute background on a news story, reporter.org could be a good place to begin looking. Created by the US-based organisation Investigative Reporters & Editors (IRE), the site is packed with journalism-related information and links. One helpful section is The Beat Page, which organises news sources according to journalistic specialisms or 'beats'. For example, at the time of writing the environment beat included links to information on the following topics: air pollution statistics; Earth viewer; Eco Net; enviro-sense; Environmental Protection Agency (EPA); global environmental options; ozone depletion; weather. Another valuable reference section, News on the Net, features links to online news services across the world.

Screenwriters and Playwrights Home Page

www.teleport.com/~cdeemer/scrwriter.html

Anyone involved in scriptwriting for TV, film or the theatre is sure to find something to interest them on this comprehensive site hosted by screenwriting guru Charles Deemer. It includes articles by Deemer himself about the craft of screenwriting, marketing, finding an agent, and so on. Details of festivals, seminars and competitions are included, and there are also links to where you can find scripts and screenplays on the web.

Screenwriter's Heaven
www.impactpc.demon.co.uk/
Compulsory viewing for screenwriters, this UK site includes links to where on the Web you can find the first draft script of *Aliens* or the shooting script of *Ferris Bueller's Day Off*. Other links include competitions, workshops, writers' software and FAQs.

Screenwriters Online
screenwriter.com/insider/news.html
Screenwriters Online describes itself as 'the only professional screen-writer's site run by major screenwriters who get their scripts and screenplays made into movies'. You have to register (give your name and other details) to get into the site, though this is free of charge. You will then get access to expert screenplay analysis, chat rooms and discussion forums, seminars with top Hollywood screenwriters, and so on.

The Slot – A Copy Editor's Guide
www.theslot.com
While obviously intended for copy editors, this is a useful site for writers as well. It is written by *Washington Post* copy editor Bill Walsh. Walsh freely admits to being opinionated – as the self-mocking sub-title 'The Curmudgeon's Style Book' indicates – but the site contains lots of useful advice and information from a man who clearly knows his (American) English. If you need advice on accents, punctuation, capitalisation, grammar or anything else writing-related, there's a good chance you'll find something here to help you.

Society of Authors
www.writers.org.uk/society/
The Society of Authors is a leading association for writers of fiction and non-fiction in the United Kingdom. Its members also include artists, illustrators, playwrights, and scriptwriters (for both radio and television). The web site gives details of the society, but also include many topics related to writing, publishing, copyright, electronic rights, and multi-media. There is a book list on various aspects of the art of writing, and hyperlinks to useful reference material and sources of information.

Society for Technical Communication
www.stc-va.org
The STC web site is aimed at technical writers, editors, designers and illustrators: professionals whose work involves communicating technical information to people who need to apply it. The site includes information on publications, employment opportunities, competitions, and more. Membership information about the Society is also included.

Society of Professional Journalists

spj.org/spjhome.htm

The US-based Society of Professional Journalists' web site includes links to dozens of journalistic resources, as well as selected articles from *Quill*, the SPJ's monthly magazine. The site also includes the Society's code of ethics for journalists, and a resource on freedom of information.

TV Writer's Home Page

www.earthlink.net/~lbrody/indexaa.html

The TV Writer's Home Page is hosted by US professional TV writer Larry Brody. This is the place to come for the lowdown on writing for Star Trek or scripting animated series such as Spider Man and The Silver Surfer. Various interesting things can be downloaded, including Brody's first draft script for a Spider Man cartoon, and a template for writing for American TV shows.

trAce Online Writing Community

trace.ntu.ac.uk

Based at Nottingham Trent University, trAce is an attempt to set up a world wide community of writers on the web. The site hosts online 'chat' meetings and discussions on topics of interest to writers, for example, 'Are writing competitions worth the effort?' The site has links to a wide range of writing-related web sites, organised into the following categories: searching the web; art and multimedia; poetry; fiction; non-fiction; scriptwriting; hypertext; literary journals and webzines; MUDs & MOOs; cyberculture and theory; miscellaneous Internet writing resources; competitions and events; conferences; and writing courses. The East Midlands Arts newsletter *Foreword* is also available on this site.

'Unaccustomed As I Am...'

speeches.com/index.shtml

This site is essential viewing for anyone who writes speeches or has to make one him or herself. It includes links to hundreds of notable speeches on the web, advice and tips on speechwriting, and tutorials on the art of writing a good speech. The site is free to browse for ideas, but to use all the resources you have to pay a small fee.

The UVic Writer's Guide

webserver.maclab.comp.uvic.ca/writersguide/starthere.html

The University of Victoria (UVic) in Canada has assembled an impressive collection of writers' resources at this site. Here you will find advice on writing in different formats, definitions of terms, a grammar guide, and a tutorial on how to present thoughts and arguments logically. A selection of links to other writing sites is included.

The Web Writer

www.geocities.com/Athens/Parthenon/8390/TOC.htm

The Web Writer is a site devoted to writers who wish to write for publication on the web. It includes information on how to set up your

Web sites for writers ....

own home page, and special considerations to bear in mind when writing for web pages.

Women Writers Project

www.stg.brown.edu/projects/wwp/wwp_home.html

On this site the Brown University Women Writers Project is assembling an electronic database of women's writing in English before 1830. The collection is still far from comprehensive, but the site also includes other, related information for those interested in this topic. There are details of an email discussion list on women's writing, and back issues of the Women Writers Project newsletter.

Writer Resources

www.seanet.com/users/warlock/writers.html

This is a comprehensive list of sites which may be of interest to fiction writers, with a brief (usually one sentence) description of each. There is a strong bias towards science fiction and fantasy.

Writers Guild

www.writers.org.uk/guild/

The Writers Guild of Great Britain represents UK writers in film, radio, television, theatre and publishing. The web site includes information about the Guild, an online newsletter, some market information, articles on the craft of writing, a list of Guild members, and links to research sites.

Writers in Electronic Residence (WIER)

www.edu.yorku.ca/WIERHOME.html

This Canadian site aims to promote the practice of writers-in-residence in schools and other institutions. During residencies writers pass on their expertise and help foster enthusiasm for writing among the students. The WIER programme aims to make writers accessible to students via the Internet, thus removing barriers created by geographical distances. At the web site you can read biographies of writers who are currently conducting electronic residencies, as well as samples of work produced, good practice advice, and numerous resources for writers, educators and publishers.

WritersNet

www.writers.net/

Sub-titled 'an Internet Resource for Writers, Editors, Publishers & Agents', this web site includes a dedicated search engine for finding internet sites devoted to particular writers. Discussion forums provide an opportunity for writers to communicate with one another, and an assignments page includes details of writing vacancies. There is also a useful section on literary agents.

Writer's Nook

www.thewritersnook.com

This is an online workshop and resource site for writers. The most popular links are to information on urban legends and hoaxes, acronyms and abbreviations, markets, and web authoring help. You may also wish to consider joining the Writer's Nook Virtual Community.

Writers Ring

www.writersring.com

This growing site for writers includes critiques, a discussion board, chat rooms, an e-zine and links to other writing-related resources.

Write Site

http://www.arcana.com/shannon/write/index.html

Part of the home page of US writer Shannon Turlington, this site includes some concise advice on writing novels and short stories. There are also links to a wide range of fiction publishers' guidelines on the web. These cover mainly genre fiction, especially science fiction, horror, mystery, children's fiction, and romance.

Young Writers' Clubhouse

www.realkids.com/club.htm

If you have a young writer in your household, point him or her at this attractive site hosted by Deborah Morris, author of *Real Kids, Real Adventures*. Morris offers non-patronising advice and encouragement to young writers. She also provides up-to-date publishing information, much of which is of equal interest to adult writers. There are competitions for young writers, and they can also read and post messages on the Young Writers' Clubhouse Bulletin board.

Zuzu's Petals

www.zuzu.com

The Zuzu's Petals Literary Resource features over 7,000 links to resources for writers, artists, performers and researchers. The links are organised in 23 main categories, including Writers, Book Publishers, Censorship, Desktop Publishing and Workshops. Each category is sub-

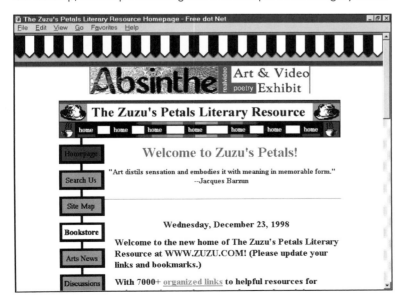

Fig. 64. Zuzu's Petals home page.

divided; for example, the Writers category includes links under the headings General Writing Resources, Plays, Fiction, Poetry, Journalism, Copyright, and so on. This site also hosts Zuzu's Petals Quarterly Online, a web-based literary magazine inviting contributions. Each issue has a different theme, for example, Arrivals and Departures.

REFERENCE RESOURCES FOR WRITERS

Amazon Bookshop (UK)

amazon.co.uk

This is the UK branch of the world's largest internet bookseller. You can search for a book by title, author or publisher. Once you have found the book or books you want, you can order online, often at a significant discount from conventional booksellers (though any discount must be set against the postal costs). Readers, authors and publishers can leave comments about their own and other people's books for other visitors to read.

Ancestry

www.ancestry.com/

If you want to research your own, or someone else's, family tree, this site would make the ideal starting point. It allows you to search across a wide range of international databases.

British Broadcasting Corporation (BBC)

www.bbc.co.uk

As you might expect the BBC has a massive site, and its news coverage (in audio, video, photographic and straight text form) is second to none. There is an archive of old news stories, background details on BBC programmes, and much, much more. The whole site is fully searchable.

British Library

www.bl.uk

As a copyright library the British Library keeps copies of every book published in the UK and many published overseas. The library also has a huge collection of journals, reports, magazines, and so on. Their web-based Portico Project is an ambitious attempt to bring many of the British Library's resources to net users. Various searches are available. OPAC 97 (Online Public Access Catalogue) is a free service which enables users to find out what material is held in the major reference and document supply collections of the Library. In many cases, it is also possible to request photocopies of documents from the library's Document Supply Centre at Boston Spa.

Buy.co.uk

www.buy.co.uk

So long as you live in the UK, this site can help you cut your overheads by revealing which of the privatised gas and electricity suppliers would offer you the best deal. The calculator takes into account the area where you live, your current annual bills, how you prefer to pay (monthly or quarterly, standard bills or direct debit), and so on. Advice on other services such as mobile phones is promised in due course.

Celebrityemail.com
www.celebrityemail.com
This site provides a means of contacting over 18,000 celebrities. It does not tell you what their email addresses are, but will forward your message on to them.

CNN
www.cnn.com
The American CNN network has a well-deserved reputation as one of the leading 24 hour news services. The web site does not let them down, with excellent audio and video feeds. When big international news stories are breaking, the CNN site can be relied on to keep you informed.

Complete Works of William Shakespeare
the-tech.mit.edu/Shakespeare/works.html
The text of all Shakespeare's plays and poems is included on this site. Obscure words, including words which have changed in meaning since Shakespeare's day, are highlighted and linked to a glossary. Other features include a Shakespeare discussion area, a list of Shakespeare resources on the net, chronological and alphabetical listings of the plays, and Bartlett's familiar quotations from Shakespeare. There are also links to other Shakespeare resources on the Internet.

CVCP ExpertNet
www.cvcp.ac.uk/expertnet.html
CVCP's ExpertNet is a resource for writers and journalists who need to track down an expert on any topic they may be researching. It is a network of university press officers. You simply send your question to the ExpertNet office by email, letter, fax or phone, and it is circulated around university press offices via the Internet. If a university employs someone with the required expertise, they will get in touch with you.

Deja News
www.dejanews.com
Deja News is the top resource for searching and browsing newsgroups on the web. With the new 'interest finder' you can enter one or more key words and see a list of newsgroups in which that topic has been discussed recently. You can also browse across a wide range of newsgroups, search for a particular group, read and post newsgroup messages, and much more.

Election Notes
www.klipsan.com/elecnews.htm
Information about parliamentary elections around the world can be accessed from this site. It includes daily news round-ups, archived results, and a calendar of forthcoming events.

Reference sources for writers

Electronic Newsstand
www.enews.com
The Electronic Newsstand includes searchable information on over 2,000 (mainly US) magazines. Reviews, information on the contents of the current issue, and links to magazine Web sites are included.

Electronic Telegraph
www.telegraph.co.uk
The electronic version of the *Daily Telegraph* was one of the first UK national newspapers to establish itself on the web. It is still one of the most popular. All the usual sections are here, from sport to international news, with links to archived stories from earlier issues.

Encyclopaedia Britannica
www.eb.com
This site includes all the articles from the hard copy *Encyclopaedia Britannica*, plus thousands more – over 72,000 in all to search or browse. They are accompanied by more than 12,000 illustrations, maps, flags and pictures. There are also links to tens of thousands of related Web sites chosen by Britannica's editors. You have to pay a modest subscription to use the site ($50 at the time of writing), but a seven-day free trial is available.

Encyclopedia.com
www.encyclopedia.com
This free site includes over 17,000 short articles from the *Concise Columbia Electronic Enyclopedia*. There is a search facility, or you can browse through the entire list of articles in alphabetical order. The site also includes links to related web sites, suggestions for further reading, and so on.

English Server
english-server.hss.cmu.edu/
The English Server, based in the English Department at Carnegie Mellon University, has links to over 20,000 works covering a wide range of interests. Topics are divided into 42 broad categories, ranging from fiction to film and television, multimedia to recipes. Visitors are encouraged to read from their collections, search for topics of interest, subscribe to their mailing lists, interact with other readers on their 'conference line', and join them in publishing quality work free of charge to internet readers.

Hansard
www.parliament.the-stationery-office.co.uk/pa/cm/cmhansrd.htm
The official record of debates and written answers in the House of Commons is available in electronic form on this rather plain-looking site. The transcript of each day's business appears promptly at noon on the following weekday.

Healthfax

www.healthfax.org.au/travind.htm

This is an Australian site designed for use by GPs. It covers the whole world, however, giving detailed advice on any special precautions and preventative measures you should take before and during a trip abroad. Consult this site before flying off to an exotic foreign destination on a special commission (or on holiday).

House of Commons Research Library

www.parliament.uk/commons/lib/research/rpintro.htm

The House of Commons Research Library prepares objective and thorough research reports on a wide range of current issues. The latest are available to download from this site.

How Do They Do That With HTML?

www.nashville.net/~carl/htmlguide/index.html

How Do They Do That With HTML? is packed with information and advice for people who want to create better-looking web pages. The site is divided into two main sections. The first part is titled 'Basic HTML and graphics', and the second is 'HTML tips and tricks'. Although the strapline says 'Answers for the novice or expert', it is not really suitable for complete beginners.

International Movie Database

www.imdb.com

This is deservedly one of the most popular sites on the web. It contains reviews, listings, commercial information and trivia on just about every film ever made. If you need background information on films, actors or the film industry, this is the place to go.

Internet Classics Archive

classics.mit.edu/titles.d.html

The Internet Classics Archive includes 441 works of classical literature by 59 different writers. Most are Greek and Roman, though there are also some Chinese and Persian. All are in English translation. Greco-Roman authors include Aeschylus, Aesop, Antiphone, Aristotle, Julius Caesar, Cicero, Epicurus, Euclid, Galen, Herodotus, Hippocrates, Homer, Lucretius, Ovid, Plato, Plutarch, Sophocles, Virgil and Xenophon. Other authors listed include Confucius, Lao-tzu and Omar Khayyam.

Independent Television News (ITN)

www.itn.co.uk

The ITN web site makes good use of the latest Internet technology to provide live video and audio reports on events making the news. As with the rival BBC web site, the content is wide and varied.

Kitchen Link

www.kitchenlink.com

An essential resource for food writers, The Kitchen Link is an enormous site featuring recipes, health information, news and tips. It also includes links to over 9,000 cookery-related sites.

Reference sources for writers

Lawrights
www.lawrights.co.uk
This site offers free electronic factsheets on UK legal processes, issues and costs. It is easy to navigate, and provides a quick introduction to a wide range of legal matters.

Liszt
www.liszt.com
As Deja News is to newsgroups, so Liszt is to Internet mailing lists. The site includes details of over 80,000 mailing lists. The main database is divided into fifteen major categories, as follows: arts, business, computers, culture, education, health, humanities, music, nature, news, politics, recreation, religion, science, social. The site is fully keyword searchable.

Multimap
www.multimap.com
This very handy site features maps of the whole UK, going as far as street map level in London. Among its many features, you can search by postcode or phone number – enter the relevant digits, and it will show you a map of the area concerned. Information on local hotels, restaurants and landmarks is also provided, and you can even get local weather reports.

Newstrawler
www.newstrawler.com/nt/nt_home.html
Newstrawler is a resource for finding out what publications across the world are saying about the big news issues. The site allows you to search the archives of hundreds of international magazines, newspapers and web-based news sources. It is free but more comprehensive than many paid-for services.

National Information Services and Systems (NISS)
www.niss.ac.uk
NISS aims to help net users around the problem of assessing the reliability of online sources. Through its Information Gateway, it gives access to a library of recommended web sites on any academic subject. NISS is aimed primarily at teachers, lecturers, students and researchers. However, it can also be a useful service for writers seeking authoritative information on any area of scholarship and learning.

Patient Information Publications
www.patient.co.uk
If you want to find out anything about medicine in the UK, this is the place to start browsing. As well as a range of informative articles, it also includes many links to other sites with detailed medical content.

Project Gutenberg
www.promo.net/pg
This site includes the text of hundreds of books now in the public domain, to be read online or downloaded for later study and analysis.

Titles covered include classic novels, poetry and reference works – from Shakespeare to T.S. Eliot, to the Bible. The site is free, but donations are welcome.

Railtrack

www.railtrack.co.uk

If you need to travel anywhere in the UK by train, this site will tell you the best route to take, what trains are available, and where you will have to change. Simple but effective, the only thing the site won't tell you is how much your journey will cost.

RecruitNet

recruitnet.guardian.co.uk

The 'Creative and Media' pages of *The Guardian* newspaper are among the best places to find out about UK writing jobs and contracts, and you can access all of them via this web site. A handy search facility allows you to specify which part of the country you are interested in and how much you want to earn. The site will then show you any current vacancies meeting these criteria.

Research It!

www.i-tools.com/researchit-com/research-it/research-it.html

Arguably one of the most useful sites on the web, Research It! (sub-title 'Your one-stop reference desk') includes links to dictionaries, currency converters, anagram solvers, translators and more.

Shopguide

www.shopguide.co.uk/

As the name suggests, Shopguide gives an overview of all the UK's online shops. Whatever you want to buy, there is a good chance that one of the sites listed here will be able to sell it to you.

Telephone Directories

www.contractjobs.com/tel/

This site provides a gateway to online telephone directories all round the world. These can save you considerable time and money on international enquiries. White pages searches, many of which allow you to search by name only, can put you in touch with the person you want in seconds.

Times, The

www.the-times.co.uk

This site gives you access to all the sections from both *The Times* and *The Sunday Times*. The site is free, though you have to register first before you can enter it. As you might expect, the in-depth news coverage is among the best you will find on the web.

University of Wolverhampton Web Search Page

www.scit.wlv.ac.uk/miscellany/search.sites.html

This site includes one of the best collections of search resources on the web. They are divided into five main categories: search engines;

Reference sources for writers ....

classified directories; meta-search engines; geographically specific resources; and subject specific gateways. Concise information is given about each of the services listed, including search options, how it presents results, where it is based, and so on. Hyperlinks will then take you to the site concerned.

Usenet Web FAQ Archive

www.faqs.org/faqs/

This site allows you to search for newsgroup FAQs (Frequently Asked Question files) by various criteria, including newsgroup, category, author, key words, and so on. FAQs can often provide invaluable background information on the topic concerned, and make fascinating browsing.

Windows To The Universe

www.ivv.nasa.gov

Windows to the Universe is an educational web site devoted to astronomy and space exploration. From the home page you can link to information on a wide range of topics at any of three different levels: beginner's, intermediate or advanced.

WWWebster Dictionary

www.m-w.com/netdict.htm

Fig. 65. Yell's home page.   This online American dictionary allows you to search for any word

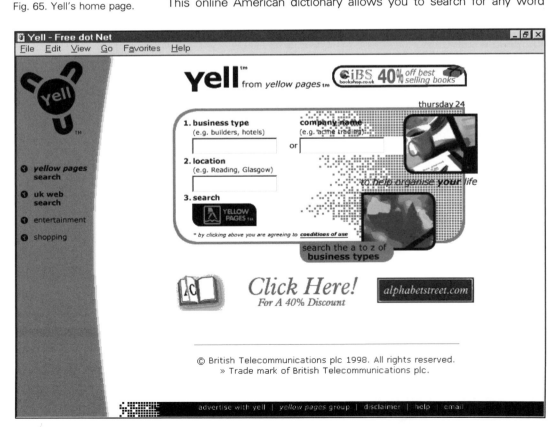

whose spelling or meaning you are uncertain of. The site also includes a thesaurus and various other features, including the Language Information Zone, Word of the Day, and Word Game of the Day.

WWW Virtual Library: Electronic Journals
www.edoc.com/ejournal/
This is a searchable database of electronic magazines and newspapers on the web. It is organised into a number of categories, including academic and reviewed journals, university and college publications, email newsletters, magazines and newspapers, business/finance, and other resources.

Yell
www.yellowpages.co.uk
The electronic version of *Yellow Pages* has all the information in the published version and more. You can search according to business type, company name or location, or browse the alphabetical index of business categories. Fast and easy to use, Yell also comes with a comprehensive film guide.

PUBLISHERS

Absey & Co.
www.absey.com
Hardcover and trade paperback fiction and non-fiction.

Acadian House Publishing
www.acadianhouse.com

Academic Press Professional
bookweb.cwis.uki.edu:8042/Books/Academic/index.html
Scientific and technical books.

Addison Wesley Longman
www.awl.co.uk
The UK site of this global educational publisher.

Agora Publishing
www.agoraworldwide.com
A book and newsletter publisher.

Allen & Unwin
www.allen-unwin.com.au/index.htm
For Australian history, military, and feminist studies.

B T Batsford Limited
www.batsford.com

Bantam, Doubleday, Dell trade books
www.bantam.com

Publishers online ....

Blackwell Publishers
www.demon.co.uk/bookshop/bw.html
Scientific and academic titles from this old-established Oxford based publisher.

Cambridge University Press
www.cup.cam.ac.uk/
Leading publisher of trade, scientific, technical, medical and academic titles.

Carlton Group
www.carlton-group.co.uk
Publishers of books on Westminster, Whitehall, executive agencies, government, public affairs, trade law, and careers.

ChemTec Publishing
www.interlog.com/~chemtec
Scientific and technical publishing.

Circlet Press
www.apocalypse.org/circlet/home.html
Publishes erotica, fantasy, and science fiction.

Del Rey Books
www.randomhouse.com/delrey/
Science fiction.

Earthscan Publications
www.earthscan.co.uk
An environmental and social science publisher.

Editions Didier Millet
www.nusantara.com/edm/
Illustrated coffee table books.

Elsevier Science
www.elsevier.nl
Leading Dutch-based international publisher of technical and scientific books and journals.

Faber and Faber
www.faber.co.uk
Old-established publisher of poetry, drama, film and literary fiction.

Glas New Russian Writing
www.birmingham.ac.uk/russian/glascover.html
For modern Russian books in English translation.

Greenhill Books
www.greenhillbooks.com
Publishers of military books for specialist readers and enthusiasts.

Greenwood Publishing Group
www.greenwood.com
An American publisher of academic, reference, trade, general interest, and professional books.

Guinness Publishing
www.guinnessrecords.com
Publishers of *The Guinness Book of Records* and other popular reference titles.

HarperCollins
www.harpercollins.co.uk
Leading publisher of popular educational and children's books, reference books, fantasy and science fiction, crime.

Headline Book Publishing
www.headline.co.uk
Publishes a range of fiction and non-fiction trade titles.

Helicon Publishing
www.helicon.co.uk
A reference publishing company specialising in electronic and multimedia products – recently acquired by the high street retailers W H Smith.

Hobsons Publishing
www.hobsons.co.uk
Specialist Cambridge-based publisher of career and educational guides.

How To Books
www.how-to-books.co.uk
Popular self-help series on careers, personal development, family reference and similar topics.

Internet Handbooks
www.internet-handbooks.co.uk
Publisher of internet guide books, in paperback. Detailed authors' guidelines can be found on the web site.

Italica Press
www.portal.com/~rww/pub_italica.html
For translations of Italian work from medieval to contemporary.

Janus Publishing Company
www.januspublishing.co.uk/
An independent publisher specialising in new and unpublished authors and books for special interest groups.

Kegan Paul International
www.demon.co.uk/keganpaul

Publishers online

Library Solutions Institute and Press
www.internet-is.com/library/
Internet books for beginners and teachers.

Macmillan Information SuperLibrary
www.mcp.com
Publishers of technical books from the Que, Que College, Sams Publishing, Alpha Books, New Riders Publishing, Hayden Books, Brady and Adobe Press imprints.

Morgan Kaufmann Publishers
market.net/literary/mkp
Computer science titles.

MIT Press
www-mitpress.mit.edu/
Massachusetts Institute of Technology – a leading USA publisher of academic, scientific and technical titles.

NESFA Press
www.transarc.com/~jmann/nesfa.html
A publisher of science fiction titles.

Orbit Books
www.orbitbooks.co.uk/
Publishers of fiction, including science fiction.

O'Reilly and Associates
www.ora.com
Computer-related publishing.

Oxford University Press
www.oup.co.uk
An old established and leading publisher of trade, scientific, technical, medical, academic, reference and children's titles.

Penguin Press
www.penguin.co.uk
Publisher of modern and classic literature, biography, popular reference and other titles.

Prentice-Hall
www.prenhall.com
Leading American publisher of technical, academic and reference books.

Productivity Press
www.ppress.com
For trade and professional titles on management and manufacturing methods.

Pulp Faction
www.pulpfact.demon.co.uk
Publishers of original contemporary fiction.

Random House
www.randomhouse.com
Leading USA publishing group which owns several popular imprints.
Publishers of trade books.

Reed Books
www.reedbooks.co.uk/home.htm

Rudra Press
www.rudra.com
A specialist publisher of yoga, spirituality, and health titles.

Saffron Editions
www.u-net.com/saffeds/
A small publisher specialising in paperback collections of short stories
by new writers.

Scandinavian University Press
www.oslonett.no/home/paul/scup.html
Publishes titles in both English and Norwegian.

Serpent's Tail
www.serpentstail.com
Publishers of popular trade books.

Scholastic
scholastic.com:2005/public/About-Scholastic.html
Publisher of children's and educational books.

Sigma Press
www.sigmapress.co.uk
For leisure, popular science and computing titles.

Siren Books
www.slicc.mcmail.com/
UK music magazines and book publishing.

Springer-Verlag
Leading German and international scientific, technical, and medical
publishers with regional-based web sites in:

Heidelberg:	www.springer.de
New York:	www.springer-ny.com
Singapore:	www.springer.com.sg

Steel Dragon Press
www.health.org/flash/steeldcat.html
For science fiction and fantasy.

Publishers online ....

Studymates
www.studymates.co.uk
Publishers of curriculum-based study and revision guides in the humanities, science and technology for students in further and higher education. Detailed authors' guidelines can be found on the web site.

Teach Yourself Books
www.teachyourself.co.uk
Old-established self-help paperbacks series.

Telos
www.telospub.com
Scientific publishers.

Thomson Publishing Company
www.thomson.com
Large publisher of business, educational and reference titles.

Tor Books
sunsite.unc.edu/ibic/Tor-homepage.html
For fantasy and science fiction.

John Wiley & Sons
www.wiley.co.uk
American publishers of scientific, technical and medical, and trade books. This is their UK web site.

Witan Books
witan-books.com

▷ *Note* – for a more comprehensive and detailed list of publishers on the internet, see *Books & Publishing on the Internet* in this series. Price £16.99 plus p&p.

SITES BY AND ABOUT WRITERS

The following sites are either hosted by or devoted to the author concerned. The contents vary considerably. Sites may include any or all of the following: examples of that author's work, bibliographies, literary criticism/appreciation, publishing news and information, bookshops, discussion forums, and links to other related sites.

Kathy Acker	members.aol.com/acker.html
Douglas Adams	www.umd.umich.edu/~nhughes/dna/
Isabel Allende	www.mojones.com/allende.html
Sherman Alexie	gcunix.gc.maricopa.edu/alexie.html
Maya Angelou	web.msu.edu/lecture/angelou.html

Isaac Asimov	www.clark.net/pub/edseiler/WWW/asimov_home_page.html
Margaret Atwood	www.web.net/owtoad
Paul Auster	www.ifs.th-darmstadt.de
Jane Austen	home.earthlink.net/austen
Julian Barnes	alexia.lis.uiuc.edu/jbrnpage.htm
Richard Beban	www.well.com/rbpoems.htm
Hakim Bey	www.uio.no/~mwatz/bey/index.html
Elizabeth Bishop	www.en.utexas.edu/bishop
Judy Blume	www.judyblume.com
Eric Bogosian	www.users.interport.net/index.html
Paul Bowles	www.garply.com/pb.html
Richard Brautigan	www.cnct.com/rich.html
Larry Brody	www.earthlink.net/~lbrody/indexaa.html
Po Bronson	users.aol.com/pobronson/humor1.htm
Anne Brontë	www.cs.cmu.edu/bronte-anne.html
Charlotte Brontë	www.stg.brown.edu/bronteov3.html
Emily Brontë	cec.wustl.edu/~jpk1
Rupert Brooke	www.bibliomania.com/Brooke
Elizabeth Barrett Browning	www.stg.brown.edu/browning2ov.html
Edgar Rice Burroughs	www.tarzan.com
William S. Burroughs	www.bigtable.com
Byron Poetry Server	rama.poly.edu/index.html
Thomas Campion	library.utoronto.ca/campion.html
Albert Camus	www.sccs.swarthmore.edu/indexa.htm
Truman Capote	www.levity.com/capote.htm
Lewis Carroll	www.students.uiuc.edu/~jbirenba/carroll.html
Gene Cartwright	members.aol.com/pgmom/genespage.html
Raymond Carver	world.std.com/~ptc/
Willa Cather	icg.harvard.edu/~cather
Raymond Chandler	www.usis.usemb.se/sft/142/sf14213.htm
Geoffrey Chaucer	www.vmi.edu/~english/chaucer.html

Writers ....

G. K. Chesterton	www.dur.ac.uk/gkc
Agatha Christie	www.nltl.columbia.edu/users1/bkyaffe/wwwac/achome.html
Tom Clancy	ourworld.compuserve.com/homepages/NWeeger/clancye.htm
Mary Higgins Clark	www.shu.edu/life/commence/95/hd3.html
Lucille Clifton	members.aol.com/clifton.html
Samuel Taylor Coleridge	www.lib.virginia.edu/etext/stc/Coleridge/stc.html
Douglas Coupland	www.coupland.com
Stephen Crane	www.en.utexas.edu/crane.html
Michael Crichton	www.globalnets.com/crichton/crichton.html
e.e. cummings	www.catalog.com/mrm/poems
Milosz Czeslaw	sunsite.unc.edu/milcov.html
Daniel Defoe	www.li.net/~scharf/defoe.html
Charles Dickens	hum.ucs.edu/dickens/index.html
James Dickey	www.wsrcc.com/pursuit.html
Emily Dickinson	lal.cs.byu.edu:80/people/black/dickinson.html
E. L. Doctorow	www.msu.edu/lecture
Hilda Doolittle	www.intac.com/hd.html
Rita Dove	www.lib.virginia.edu/dove.html
Arthur Conan Doyle	www.cis.ohiostate.edu/hypertext/faq/usenet/books/holmes/illustrated/faq.html
Finley Peter Dunne	web.syr.edu/~fjzwick/dooley/
Marguerite Duras	www.uta.fi/~trkisa/duras/duras.html
Umberto Eco	www4.ncsu.edu/eos/users/m/mcmesser/www/eco.html
Lars Eighner	www.io.com/~eighner
T. S. Eliot	virtual.park.uga.edu/eliot.taken.html
Harlan Ellison	www.teleport.com/~mzuzel/
Paul Eluard	www.lm.com/eluard.html
Philip Jose Farmer	www.mindspring.com/~ledzep/
William Faulkner	www.mcsr.olemiss.edu/~egjbp/faulkner/faulkner.html
Ian Fleming	www.mcs.net/fleming.html

Dick Francis	www.math.ru/ru/members/hohlov/hobby/books/f/
Anne Frank	glyphs.com/millpop/95/annefrank.html
Carolyn Forche	osf1.gmu.edu/index.html
Kahlil Gibran	impact.civil.columbia.edu/gibran.html
Nikki Giovanni	athena.english.vt.edu/Nikki_Giovanni
Allen Ginsberg	nickel.ucs.indiana.edu/ginsberg.html
Ray Girvan	www.users.zetnet.co.uk/rgirvan/
Goethe	members.aol.com/goethe.html
Sue Grafton	www.suegrafton.com
Robert Graves	www.nene.ac.uk/graves.html
Angelina Weld Grimke	www.sappho.com/a_grimke.htm
John Grisham	www.bdd.com/grisham
Parnell Hall	pathfinder.com/twep/mysterious_press/hall/
Robert Hass	www.diacenter.org/intrhass.html
Nathaniel Hawthorne	www.tiac.net/users/eldred/nh/hawthorne.html
Seamus Heaney	sunsite.unc.edu/heaney-cov.html
Robert A. Heinlein	www.clark.net/pub/ahasuer/heinlein/heinlein.html
Frank Herbert	www.princeton.edu/~cgilmore/dune/
Langston Hughes	www.ecnet.net/users/mujdh5/hughes.htm
Richard Hugo	members.aol.com/hugo.html
David Ignatow	www.cais.com/ignatow
Henry James	www.tiac.net/users/eldred/hjj/dm/daisy1.html
James Joyce	astro.ocis.temple.edu/~callahan/joyce.html
Thomas Keneally	bookweb.cwis.uci.edu/Keneally.html
Jack Kerouac	www.charm.net/~brooklyn/LitKicks.html
Ken Kesey	www.charm.net/KeseyBiblio.html
Omar Khayyam	www-leland.stanford.edu/omar.html
Stephen King	wwwcsif.cs.ucdavis.edu/~pace/king.html
Dean Koontz	www.dkoontz.com
Milan Kundera	www.georgetown.edu/kundera.html
Louis L'Amour	www.accessnow.com/ll/welcome.html
D. H. Lawrence	www.cs.berkeley.edu/lawrence

Writers

Doris Lessing	tile.net/lessing/
C.S. Lewis	www.cache.net/~john/cslewis/index.html
Jack London	sunsite.berkeley.edu/London/
Amy Lowell	www.sappho.com/a_lowell.htm
Audre Lorde	stripe.colorado.edu/lorde_toc.html
Anne McCaffrey	arrogant.itc.icl.ie/AnneMcCaffrey.html
Carson McCullers	cathouse.org:80/Literature/CarsonMcCullers/
Terry McMillan	www.bookwire.com/mcmillan.html
Katherine Mansfield	www.buffnet.net/kmansfld.htm
Charlotte Mew	www.sappho.com/c_mew.htm
Jack Micheline	www.jackmicheline.com
Marianne Moore	www.cwrl.utexas.edu/mm.html
Toni Morrison	www.luminarium.org/tonimorrison
Edwin Muir	ourworld.compuserve.com/edwmuir0.htm
Pablo Neruda	www.uic.edu/neruda.html
Anais Nin	www.dol.com/nin
Eugene O'Neill	www.columbia.edu/oneill
Mary Oliver	www.geocities.com/oliver.htm
George Orwell	www.levity.com/orwell.htm
Dorothy Parker	www.suck-my-big.org/poems
Kenneth Patchen	ourworld.compuserve.com/Patchen
Marge Piercy	www.capecod.net/~tmpiercy
Li Po	www.physics.wisc.edu/Li_Po
Edgar Allan Poe	www.cs.umu.se/~dpcnn/eapoe/ea_poe.html
Rilke	www.wmich.edu/Hall.rilke.html
Theodore Roethke	uts.cc.utexas.edu/roethke.html
Christina Rossetti	www.stg.brown.edu/crov2.html
Antoine de Saint-Exupery	www.sas.upenn.edu/exupery
J.D. Salinger	www.stardot.com/holden
George Sand	www.eden.com/gs_home.html
Carl Sandburg	www.columbia.edu/sandburg
Sappho	www.sappho.com/sappho.htm

Dr Seuss	klinzhai.iuma.com/~drseuss/seuss/
Anne Sexton	www.crl.com/sexton.html
William Shakespeare	the-tech.mit.edu/Shakespeare/works.html
John Steinbeck	www.mbay.net/~etrosow
August Strindberg	www.jmk.su.se/index.html
Amy Tan	www.luminarium.org/amytan
J.R.R. Tolkien	www.lights.com/tolkien/timeline.html
Tolstoy	users.aol.com/Tolstoy28/tolstoy.htm
Wu Tsao	www.sappho.com/wu_tsao.htm
Mark Twain	web.syr.edu/~~fjzwick/twainwww.html
Paul Valery	www.lm.com/valery.html
Kurt Vonnegut	www.geocities.com/kv_essays.html
Eudora Welty	www.cssc.olemiss.edu/homepage.html
Walt Whitman	www.cc.columbia.edu/whitman
Oscar Wilde	haven.ios.com/~wordup/wilde/dorgray.html
Jeanette Winterson	home8.swipnet.se/~w-83331
Richard Wright	www.itvs.org/RW
Tom Wolfe	web.msu.edu/lecture/wolfe.html
W.B. Yeats	www.geocities.com/yeats_index.html
Roger Zelazny	www.itmm.com/scott/zelazny/index.shtml

Appendix: Internet access providers

The following is a list of the most popular and best known internet access providers in the UK. If you are curious to find out more about access providers worldwide, see the note at the end of this list.

AOL
www. uk.aol.com
America OnLine – the biggest internet access provider in the world. It offers its own services aside from the internet itself, and if you require 24 hour access it is more expensive than most.
Tel: (0800) 279 1234

BT Internet
www. btinternet.com
A service of British Telecommunications PLC. It is making a pitch for the educational market.
Tel: (0800) 800 001

CIX
www.cix.co.uk
Tel: (0845) 355 9050

ClaraNET
www.clara.net
Tel: (0800) 358 2828

CompuServe
www.compuserve.co.uk
Like AOL, CompuServe is noteworthy for its additional members' services, in addition to linking you to the wider internet.
Tel: (0990) 000 200

Demon
www.demon.net
A pioneering UK access provider, which in 1998 lost its independence by becoming a subsidiary of Scottish Telecom. You need the Turnpike Suite for email and newsgroups.
Tel: (0181) 371 1234

Direct Connection
www.dircon.net
Tel: (0800) 072 0000

Enterprise
www.enterprise. net
Tel: (01624) 677666

FreeDotNet
www.thefree.net
Tel: (0181) 938 3338

Global Internet
www.global. net. uk
Tel: (0870) 909 8041

Microsoft (MSN)
www.uk.msn.com
Bill Gates wants to be in the internet access provider market, too. The service is highly automated – don't expect much human contact. Its browser of course is Internet Explorer.
Tel: (0345) 002 000

NetDirect
www.netdirect.net.uk
Tel: (0181) 293 7000

U-Net
www.u-net.net
Tel: (0845) 3000448

UUNET (Pipex Dial)
www.uk.uu.net
Tel: (0500) 567 000

Virgin Net
www.virgin.net
Part of the Richard Branson empire. One of Virgin's advantages is its helpful 24 hour a day helpline.
Tel: (0500) 558 800

Zetnet Services
www.zetnet.co. uk
Tel: (01595) 696 667

▷ Note – there are more than 200 internet access providers in the UK today, some 4,000 in the United States, and more than 10,000 world wide. Many are small specialist or local operations of one kind or another. A comprehensive list of UK providers appears in some of the monthly glossy internet magazines. If you are concerned about the threat to your privacy in the UK, or just curious to find out more, you can explore internet access providers world wide at this impressive 'list of lists'. With falling phone rates everywhere, the world is your oyster:

www. herbison.com/herbison/iap_meta_list. html

Glossary of internet terms

Applet – A small application written in the programming language Java. It is most often used to produce a ticker-tape effect running across the bottom of your screen.

Archie – A search tool which enables you to look for files stored on hundreds of anonymous FTP sites across the internet. You can access Archie via the web at:

cuiwww.unige.ch/archieplexform.html

ASCII – American Standard Code for Information Interchange. This is a language understood by all computers. It is the one in which standard email messages are transmitted.

Attachments – Word processing and other non-ASCII files which are sent as part of an email message. Attached files must first be converted to a format which can be transmitted across the internet using a method such as MIME. You don't normally need to worry about this, as most modern email programs handle this format automatically.

Bandwidth – This term is generally used to describe how much data you can send through a connection at any one time. Text-only emails use up very little bandwidth, while video consumes large amounts.

Bit – Bit stands for binary digit. This is the smallest unit of data that can be handled by a computer. A bit can be either a one or a zero. It takes eight bits (a byte) to represent one character such as a letter or a number.

Bookmarks – This is the term used in the Netscape Navigator browser for your quick reference list of favourite web sites.

Browser – A browser is a special program which enables your computer to view web pages and other internet resources. The two best-known browsers are Netscape Navigator and Microsoft Internet Explorer.

Bulletin board – An electronic notice board, often hosted on a small personal computer. Visitors can log on to a bulletin board by dialling the appropriate phone number using their modem. They can then read messages others have posted, and leave messages of their own. Bulletin boards have to some extent been superseded by the internet.

Byte – A byte is a set of bits which represents a single character, for example a letter or a number. There are eight bits in a byte, for example 00110110. A kilobyte (KB) contains 1,024 bytes of data; a megabyte

(MB) has 1,048,576 bytes; and a gigabyte (GB) has 1,000 megabytes.

Chat – A chat program allows you to communicate online with one or more people in real time. You type your questions or comments, and other people's responses then appear on screen as you watch. Special software may be required to get the most from chat programs, though many modern services work quite happily with an ordinary browser. See also **IRC**.

CD-ROM – This stands for Compact Disk, Read-Only Memory. A CD-ROM can store the equivalent of 1,500 ordinary floppy disks. They are currently the most popular carriers of multimedia programs that feature audio, video and graphics as well as text.

Communities – This term is used in various ways on the internet. Service providers such as CompuServe organise their discussion forums under a small number of communities. There are 14 of these in CompuServe at the time of writing, each representing a particular area of interest (such as business, travel, news, education). Some web sites host so-called writers' communities. These generally include reference material, and facilities such as chat rooms, discussion forums and some means of displaying members' work.

Cyberspace – This word was first coined by science fiction writer William Gibson in his 1984 novel *Neuromancer*. It is now used to refer to any site which can be accessed electronically. If your computer is connected to the internet, then it too exists in cyberspace.

Dial-up connection – If you have a dial-up connection to the internet, it means you have to make a phone call to get connected. This method is slower than connecting directly to the internet backbone, but is straightforward and allows access from anywhere with a phone connection.

Domain – This is part of the naming system of the internet which specifies each computer's nature and location. Addresses are written as a series of names separated by full stops. Some of the most common domain names include the following:

.ac.uk	academic and research (mainly universities)
.com	commercial
.co.uk	company
.edu	education (USA)
.gov	government or other public body
.net	network resource
.org	organisation
.sch	school

Download – To transfer a program or other information from the internet to your computer.

Glossary of internet terms ....

DVD – Stands for either Digital Video Disk or Digital Versatile Disk. DVDs have a higher storage capacity than CD-ROMs, and are eventually expected to supersede them.

Electronic bookshop – A web site offering books for sale, with payment online by credit or debit card. The largest electronic bookshop currently operating in the UK is Amazon.co.uk.

Email – The simplest of internet services, email allows you to communicate with other internet users across the world. It is fast, convenient and should never cost you more than the price of a short local phone call. See also **attachment**.

E-zine – Sometimes shortened to zines, these are magazines published in electronic format (usually on the internet). One example of a writing-related e-zine is *Bricolage*, at:

bricolage.bel-epa.com/

FAQ – This stands for Frequently Asked Questions. FAQ files are most commonly found in newsgroups, but many web sites now have them as well. They are a compendium of commonly asked questions and answers on a particular topic. You can see a large selection of FAQs at:

ftp://src.doc.ic.ac.uk/usenet/news-info/

Favorites – This is the term used in Microsoft Internet Explorer for your quick reference list of favourite web sites. If you use Netscape, the equivalent term is **bookmarks**.

Flaming – This refers to the practice of sending a torrent of derogatory emails ('flames') to another internet user, generally a person who has breached the rules of good netiquette.

Forums – A forum is an internet discussion area. The term is generally used to refer to internet bulletin boards and similar facilities which enable visitors to read other people's messages and post their own. Chat rooms, in contrast, allow users to communicate with one another in real time.

Freeware – Computer programs which can be obtained and used for any length of time without charge.

FTP – File Transfer Protocol, the method by which files are transferred across the internet. Modern browsers can handle FTP without the need for any other special software.

Gigabyte – A measure of computer storage capacity. A gigabyte (GB) is equivalent to 1,000 megabytes.

Hacker – Someone who deliberately attempts to break through a computer security system. Some hackers are simply pranksters, but others are professional criminals.

Hits – Term loosely used to describe the number of visitors to a web site. Strictly speaking, it refers to the number of times items from a web page (e.g. text, graphics, applets) have been downloaded.

Home page – Strictly speaking, a home page is the entry point of a web site. When you enter a URL in your browser, or follow a hyperlink, the site's home page will normally appear on your screen first. Increasingly, however, the term is used to refer to a whole web site.

Hotlists – Term used to describe a list of popular or recommended web sites, usually on a particular theme. On the web, hotlists invariably include hyperlinks to take you straight to the sites concerned.

HTML – This stands for HyperText Mark-up Language. It is the programming language in which all web pages are written (with other languages such as Java being used to provide additional features and effects).

Hyperlinks – Sometimes called 'hot links' or just plain 'links', these are special features of web pages. A hyperlink takes you instantly to another web page when you click your mouse over it. The presence of a hyperlink is often indicated on screen by underlining. Your mouse pointer will change shape when the cursor is positioned over one.

Hypertext – This describes text in web documents which includes hyperlinks to other documents (or to another place in the same document). Hypertext may be used for explanations of unfamiliar terms, for references, or for more detailed articles on a particular topic for those wanting in-depth information. Hypertext is also used in interactive fiction, where the choices made by a reader determine the progress of the narrative.

IAP – Internet access provider. A company or other organisation which provides people with the means of getting on the internet, generally for a fee.

Internet – An international network of computers set up to exchange information via telephone lines and modems. It is sometimes referred to as 'the net' for short.

Intranet – A network of linked computers within a company or organisation. Many intranets use the same software and hardware that are used for internet access. However, intranet users may have only limited access to and from the internet (for example, email only), or no access at all.

IRC – Internet Relay Chat. This is a system allowing users to communicate with one another in real time via their computer keyboards. It has been described as the CB radio of the internet. You need special, dedicated software to make use of IRC, and it is likely to be superseded by web-based chat services.

ISP – Internet service provider. This term is sometimes used interchangeably with IAP. Strictly speaking, however, it should be applied only to services such as AOL which provide a range of services for their members in addition to internet access. All ISPs are also IAPs, but the opposite is not true.

Java – A special programming language which can be used to create effects such as ticker-tape messages on web pages.

Listserv – The most common system for running internet mailing lists.

Lurking – The practice of reading postings in a newsgroup or mailing list without contributing anything yourself. It sounds undesirable; but in reality lurking is perfectly acceptable and often the best way to get a feel for the unwritten rules and conventions of a group before venturing your first contribution.

Mailing list – Internet mailing lists provide a simple way of sending the same email message to any number of people at the same time. They are used to send regular news and information to people sharing a common interest.

MIME – Multipurpose Internet Mail Extensions. Nowadays this is the most common way in which non-ASCII files are converted to a suitable format for the internet, so that they can be sent as attachments to ordinary emails.

Mirror – A mirror is a copy of a web or FTP site on another server (host computer). The aim is to reduce the load on the original server by offering users a choice of sites from which to access the information they require.

Modem – Modem stands for MOdulator/DEModulator. It is a device which enables your computer to communicate with other computers and access the internet via an ordinary phone line.

Multimedia – This term covers forms of communication which make use of a variety of media: not only text, but also graphics, photographs, sound, video, animations and so on.

Netiquette – The etiquette of the internet, the unwritten rules - though various people have written their own versions - of acceptable and unacceptable online behaviour. One example is that it is usually considered impolite to write emails in ALL CAPITALS. This is the internet equivalent of shouting.

Newsgroup – Newsgroups are the bulletin boards of the internet. Anyone accessing a newsgroup can read messages other people have sent in. If they wish, they can then reply to these messages or post other messages of their own. There are many thousands of newsgroups divided into families. Each of these shares a common prefix such as misc, rec or alt, for example alt.astrology or misc.writing.

Newsreader – A program especially designed to help you find your way around newsgroups. Browsers such as Netscape Navigator will allow you to read and write to newsgroups, but a dedicated newsreader such as Free Agent makes the task easier.

Online – Being connected to the internet. The opposite is 'offline'.

Plug-in – Add-on extras for browsers. Plug-ins may be required before you can benefit from the latest technology for receiving video clips or live audio across the net. Plug-ins can be downloaded over the internet; many are free, but some have to be paid for.

Point of presence – Often abbreviated to PoP, this is a phone number given out by an internet access provider for people to dial in on their modems. Many providers now use 0845 numbers to allow their subscribers local rate access from anywhere in the country.

Protocol – Basically, this means an agreed way for two computers to communicate with one another. One example is point-to-point protocol (PPP). This allows a computer to use a normal phone line to connect with the internet. Another example is Telnet, a protocol which enables one computer to act as though it has become a dumb terminal (monitor and keyboard only) of another.

Search engine – This is a tool which searches through the internet to find references to a specific phrase or word. Some of the best known search engines are Alta Vista, Lycos and Excite. Another information-finding tool is an 'internet directory' such as Yahoo.

Server – A powerful computer which is connected to a network and makes services and data available to other users. All web home pages must be hosted on a server for other internet users to be able to access them.

Shareware – Software you can test out for a limited period (often 30 days) before deciding whether or not to buy. If you wish to continue using a shareware program after this trial period, you should register with the program's author.

Smiley – A smiley is a form of punctuation which, viewed side on, looks vaguely like a human face. These 'emoticons' are used in emails and newsgroup postings to show the sender's emotional state, for example:

happy   :-)   sad   :-(

Glossary of internet terms ....

Spamming – Slang term for posting the same, unsolicited message to a large number of email addresses or newsgroups at the same time. Spamming is often used for advertising purposes. It is highly unpopular among net users, because it can be intrusive and waste people's time.

Surfing the net – Slang term for casually exploring the internet. Surfing means clicking on hyperlinks and travelling from one site to the next as fancy takes you. Surfing the net can be fun, until your phone bill arrives!

Telnet – A method for connecting your computer to another so that it appears your computer becomes a dumb terminal (keyboard and monitor only) of that machine. Telnet once made up the majority of internet traffic, but it has now generally been superseded by the web. Most modern browsers, however, will handle Telnet if required.

URL – Standing for Uniform Resource Locator, a URL is the electronic 'address' of a web site. For example, the full URL of the search engine Excite is

http://www.excite.com

The URL provides the information your browser needs in order to access the site concerned.

Usenet – This is the system of newsgroups on the internet. Usenet preceded the world wide web, but unlike some other internet protocols (such as Telnet) it is still going strong.

Virus – A virus is a special type of program which has been created for just two purposes. One is to replicate itself and pass undetected to other people's machines. The other is to cause some form of mischief (or worse) when it is activated. All computer-users should install a virus-checker on their machines and update it regularly.

World wide web – known as 'the web' for short, this has become the largest and most technologically sophisticated part of the internet. Web pages can include text, graphics, photographs, sound and video, animations, and much more. Web pages also have hyperlinks – text or images which, when you click your mouse over them, instantly transport you to another web site.

Further reading and reference

. . . .

Books & Publishing on the Internet
Roger Ferneyhough
Internet Handbooks UK, 1999
www.internet-handbooks.co.uk

Carol Vorderman's Guide to the Internet
Carol Vorderman and Rob Young
Prentice-Hall Europe, 1998
www.prenhall.com

The Complete Idiot's Guide to the Internet: UK Edition 1999
Rob Young
Prentice-Hall USA, 1998
www.prenhall.com

Creating a Web Site
Bruce Durie
How To Books, 1998
www.how-to-books.co.uk

Doing Business on the Internet
Graham Jones
How To Books, 1997
www.how-to-books.co.uk

Find it on the Internet
Kye Valongo
Internet Handboks UK, 1999
www.internet-handbooks.co.uk

HTML 4 for Dummies
Ed Tittel and Steve James
IDG Books Worldwide, 1998
www.mispress.com

News & Magazines on the Internet
Michael Newman
Internet Handbooks UK, 1999
www.internet-handbooks.co.uk

Teach Yourself the Internet
Mac Bride
Teach Yourself Books, 1998
www.teachyourself.co.uk

Further reading and reference ....

The Internet 4.0: The Rough Guide 1999
Angus J. Kennedy
Rough Guides Limited, London, 1998
roughguides.com

The Internet Handbook for Writers, Researchers & Journalists
Mary McGuire, Linda Stilborne, Melinda McAdams and Laurel Hyatt
Trifolium Books, Toronto, Canada, 1997
www.pubcouncil.ca/trifolium

The UK Internet Book
Sue Schofield
Addison-Wesley Longman
www.awl.co.uk

The Writers Internet Handbook
Timothy Maloy
Allworth Press, New York, USA, 1997
www.allworth.com

Using the Internet
Graham Jones
How To Books, 1998
www.howtobooks.co.uk

Useful addresses

Arts For Everyone (A4E) Unit
The Arts Council of England
14 Great Peter Street
London
SW1P 3NQ
Tel: (0171) 973 6582
Application form hotline: (0990) 100344
Unit which deals with applications for National Lottery funding under
the Arts for Everyone scheme.

Association for Business Sponsorship of the Arts (ABSA)
2 Chester Street
London
SW1A 7BB
Tel: (0171) 235 9781
Will advise on obtaining private and business sponsorship for arts
projects. Also has a network of regional offices.

Author-Publisher Network
12 Mercers
Hawkhurst
Kent
TN18 4LH
Tel: (01580) 753346
Provides a forum for writers who wish to publish their own work, in
electronic as well as traditional media.

Authors' Licensing and Collecting Society (ALCS)
74 New Oxford Street
London
WC1A 1EF
Tel: (0171) 255 2034
Web site: www.alcs.co.uk
Collects and distributes certain collective payments to writers,
including reprography and some electronic rights.

Chartered Institute of Journalists
2 Dock Offices
Surrey Quays Road
London
SE16 2XU
Tel: (0171) 252 1187
Professional organisation open to writers, broadcasters and
journalists in all media.

Useful addresses for writers

Comedy Writers' Association of Great Britain
61 Parry Road
Ashmore Park
Wolverhampton
West Midlands
WV11 2PS
Tel: (01902) 722729
International organisation which assists and promotes the work of comedy writers, especially (but not exclusively) in television.

Crime Writers' Association
60 Drayton Road
Kings Heath
Birmingham
B14 7LR
Association for professional crime writers (though others are welcome to join as Associate members).

The English Association
University of Leicester
University Road
Leicester
LE1 7RH
Tel: (0116) 252 3982
Organisation which supports English teaching in schools, colleges and universities. It aims to promote the appreciation of English language and literature across the world.

The Federation of Worker Writers and Community Publishers (FWWCP)
PO Box 540
Burslem
Stoke-on-Trent
Staffordshire
ST6 6DR
Tel: (01782) 822327
An association of writers' groups committed to writing and publishing based on working class experience and creativity.

The Library Association
7 Ridgmount Street
London
WC1E 7AE
Tel: (0171) 636 7543
Professional association for librarians and others concerned with information management.

National Association of Writers Groups
The Arts Centre
Biddick Lane
Washington

Tyne & Wear
NE38 2AB
Association which aims to further the interests of writers groups
throughout the UK. Produces a bi-monthly newsletter.

National Association of Writers in Education (NAWE)
PO Box 1
Sheriff Hutton
York YO6 7YU
Tel: (01653) 618429
Association representing writers who work in schools, colleges and
community groups. Publishes an annual directory of writers available
for such work.

National Union of Journalists
Acorn House
314 Gray's Inn Road
London
WC1X 8DP
Tel: (0171) 278 7916
Web site: www.gn.apc.org/media/nuj.html
Represents journalists in publishing, print and broadcasting.

PEN
7 Dilke Street
London
SW3 4JE
Tel: (0171) 352 6303
International organisation which seeks to protect writers' freedom of
expression.

The Poetry Society
22 Betterton Street
London
WC2H 9BU
Tel: (0171) 240 4810
Web site: www.poetrysociety.co.uk
Sponsors of the prestigious annual National Poetry Competition, and
promoters of poetry and poetry events across the UK.

The Society for Storytelling
Contact: Joan Barr (Secretary)
Society for Storytelling
8 Bert Allen Drive
Old Leake
Boston
Lincs PE22 9LG
Organisation supporting and representing storytellers (fiction writers
who perform their work to an audience rather than publishing in book
form).

Useful addresses for writers

The Society of Authors
84 Drayton Gardens
London
SW10 9SB
Tel: (0171) 373 6642
Web site: www.writers.org.uk/society/
Independent trade union representing and supporting authors and scriptwriters.

Society of Freelance Editors and Proofreaders (SFEP)
Mermaid House
1 Mermaid Court
London
SE1 1HR
Tel: (0171) 403 5141
Web site: www.sfep.demon.co.uk
Professional organisation serving and representing freelance proofreaders and editors.

Society of Women Writers and Journalists
110 Whitehall Road
London
E4 6DW
Tel: (0181) 529 0886
Association of women engaged in journalism. Services include monthly lectures, advice and a quarterly journal.

Way Ahead Electronic Publishing
5 Woodlands
Tebworth
Nr Leighton Buzzard
Bedfordshire
LU7 9QR
Tel: (01582) 877822
Publishers of the electronic tutorials Creative Writing, Short Story Acumen, Make Your Holidays Pay, and so on.

The Writers Bureau
Sevendale House
7 Dale Street
Manchester
M1 1JB
Tel: (0161) 228 2362
Web site: www.writersbureau.com
The UK's largest correspondence school offering commercial courses in freelance writing.

The Writers' Guild of Great Britain
430 Edgware Road
London
W2 1EH

Tel: (0171) 723 8074
Web site: www.writers.org.uk/guild/
Organisation representing writers in film, radio, television, theatre
and publishing.

REGIONAL ARTS BOARDS

Regional Arts Boards support writers in their region with
publications, courses, advice on funding, and in some cases grant
aid. RABs cover England only; in Scotland, Wales and Ireland,
contact the relevant Arts Council initially.

East Midlands Arts
Mountfields House
Epinal Way
Loughborough
Leicestershire
LE11 0QE
Tel: (01509) 218292
Covers Leicestershire, Nottinghamshire, Derbyshire (excluding the
High Peak district) and Northamptonshire.

Eastern Arts Board
Cherry Hinton Hall
Cambridge
CB1 4DW
Tel: (01223) 215355
Covers Bedfordshire, Cambridgeshire, Essex, Hertfordshire, Norfolk,
Suffolk and Lincolnshire.

London Arts Board
Elme House
3rd Floor, 133 Long Acre
London
WC2E 9AF
Tel: (0171) 240 1313
Covers the 32 London boroughs and the City of London.

North West Arts Board
4th Floor
12 Harter Street
Manchester
M1 6HY
Tel: (0161) 228 3062
Covers Cheshire, Greater Manchester, Merseyside, Lancashire and
the High Peak district of Derbyshire.

Northern Arts Board
9-10 Osborne Terrace
Jesmond
Newcastle-upon-Tyne

Regional arts boards...

NE2 1NZ
Tel: (0191) 281 6334
Covers Cleveland, Cumbria, Durham, Northumberland and Tyne &
Wear.

South East Arts
10 Mount Ephraim
Tunbridge Wells
Kent
TN4 8AS
Tel: (01892) 515210
Covers Kent, Surrey, East and West Sussex (excluding the London
boroughs).

South West Arts
Bradninch Place
Gandy Street
Exeter
Devon
EX4 3LS
Tel: (01392) 218188
Covers Avon, Cornwall, Devon, much of Dorset, Gloucestershire and
Somerset.

Southern Arts
13 St Clement Street
Winchester
Hampshire
SO23 9DQ
Tel: (01962) 855099
Covers Berkshire, Buckinghamshire, Hampshire, Isle of Wight,
Oxfordshire, Wiltshire and South East Dorset.

West Midlands Arts
82 Granville Street
Birmingham
B1 2LH
Tel: (0121) 631 3121
Covers West Midlands county, Staffordshire, Hereford and
Worcester, Warwickshire and Shropshire.

Yorkshire & Humberside Arts
21 Bond Street
Dewsbury
West Yorkshire
WF13 1AY
Tel: (01924) 455555
Covers the counties of Yorkshire (South, North and West) and
Humberside.

THE ARTS COUNCIL

The Arts Council of England
14 Great Peter Street
London
SW1P 3NQ
Tel: (0171) 333 0100

The Arts Council, Ireland
An Chomhairle Ealaion
70 Merrion Square
Dublin 2
Ireland
Tel: (00 353) 1 6611840

The Arts Council of Northern Ireland
185 Stranmillis Road
Belfast
BT9 5DU
Tel: (01232) 381591

Scottish Arts Council
12 Manor Place
Edinburgh
EH3 7DD
Tel: (0131) 226 6051

The Arts Council of Wales
Holst House
9 Museum Place
Cardiff
CF1 3NX
Tel: (01222) 394711

Index

Index . . . .